STALKING MUNTJAC

STALKING MUNTJAC

A Complete Guide

Graham Downing

Quiller

First published in the UK in 2014
by Quiller, an imprint of Quiller Publishing Ltd

British Library Cataloguing-in-Publication Data
A catalogue record for this book is available from the British Library

ISBN 978 1 84689 185 4

Designed and typeset by Arabella Ainslie

All photographs are the copyright of the author unless credited otherwise

Printed in China

Quiller

An imprint of Quiller Publishing Ltd
Wykey House, Wykey, Shrewsbury, SY4 1JA
Tel: 01939 261616 Fax: 01939 261606
E-mail: info@quillerbooks.com
Website: www.quillerpublishing.com

CONTENTS

INTRODUCTION

It is early March. The hazel copse is hung with dusty yellow catkins and the bursting leaves of honeysuckle glow in the early morning sunshine. A blackbird sings as if to celebrate the returning spring and from high above in the tall timber comes the staccato drumming of a woodpecker.

The old buck warms himself in the quiet sunshine. This is his territory. He knows every coppice stool and each of the big oaks beyond. He knows the paths and tracks through the blackthorn scrub, the rabbit warren in the sandy bank and the crab apple tree that fed him late into the autumn.

His ancestors chose well when they discovered this place twenty summers ago. There were no other deer in the woods back in those days and, having tracked the hedges and spinneys from across the valley, the canny doe that was his great, great grandmother stayed and settled. Now, as well as muntjac, there are roe and even the occasional red hind drifting through from the far, dark forest. But this is muntjac country. The buck lowers his head, barks a proprietorial bark, and from somewhere on the edge of the great wood, there comes a bark in reply.

Muntjac have been a phenomenally successful species over the past few decades. Plucked from their oriental homeland by nineteenth century collectors, they have shown themselves to be supremely adaptable to our temperate climate and they have settled readily into the busy landscape of southern and eastern England, to the delight of some and to the concern and consternation of many others. But, as with all our deer, muntjac have no natural predators and if they are to be prevented from coming into conflict with our own use of the countryside or upsetting the delicately poised balance of nature, muntjac must be managed. For those charged with managing muntjac, the species is a challenging match: it is small, hard to spot and it demands quick thinking and fast reflexes if it is to be hunted successfully.

For me, muntjac add interest to the countryside. Whether it is the presence of fresh slot marks around the farm as I walk the dogs in the morning or the sound of barking under the starlight of a crisp winter's night, I enjoy their presence. For the past fifteen years I have also enjoyed hunting them, and the more I have done so, the more I have come to respect this species. Like every branch of field sports, successful muntjac stalking is a constant learning process, and I hope that some of the comments and recollections which I have gathered together in this book provide assistance to others who, like me, have been bitten by the muntjac bug.

I would like to pay tribute to those who have helped me, and in particular to Norma Chapman and Arnold Cooke for sharing the results of their research; to Chris Rogers for his expertise in trophy assessment and measuring; to Charles Smith-Jones for his unshakeable enthusiasm for all things muntjac; to Professor Jimmy Simpson for his comments on foot injury and antler formation and of course to my wife Ronnie for sharing with me her own love for the creatures from the perspective of both stalker and cook.

Thanks also to George Lawrence-Brown for his fabulous pencil drawings, to Lloyd French, David Mason, Matthew Peaster, Sue Westlake-Guy, Craig Churchill and Terry Richards for allowing me to use their lovely photographs and to the British Deer Society for supplying the distribution maps and for their support and assistance.

Although many may wish that it was not, the muntjac is here to stay. I hope that this book helps those who come into contact with it, and above all the deer stalking fraternity, to learn and understand a little more about the species, to respect it as a challenging quarry, to manage it humanely and responsibly, and even to appreciate having it around them in the landscape of lowland England.

Graham Downing

Chediston, 2014

The muntjac is one of the most successful introduced mammals to have become established in Britain's countryside

THE STORY OF MUNTJAC IN BRITAIN

Muntjac deer have become such a common sight in southern England, whether creeping across a forest ride at dawn, scrumping apples in a cottage garden or caught in the headlights on the verge of a busy suburban dual carriageway, that they might be thought a natural component of Britain's wildlife. They are not native to these shores, of course, but they do have the distinction of belonging to that exclusive club of introduced exotic species that have made the leap from captivity into the wild and have then gone on to become successfully naturalised. Indeed, the muntjac may be regarded as one of the most successful introduced mammals to have become established in Britain's countryside.

Origins and Introduction

So where did the story start? The origins of the *Muntiacinae* to which belongs Reeves's muntjac (*Muntiacus reevesi*), the species which can be found wild in Britain, go back some six million years to the Pliocene epoch when five separate tribes emerged within the deer family, the *Cervidae*, possibly as a result of geological and climatic change. In prehistoric times animals related to the ancestors of modern muntjac occurred in what is now western Europe, but today's representatives of the muntjac family are to be found in south east Asia, from China and India through Myanmar (Burma), Cambodia and Vietnam to Indonesia. Until quite recently there were believed to be six species: the Reeves's, Indian, Roosevelt's, Fea's, Bornean Yellow and Black muntjac; but as recently as the 1990s a further four have been identified in the remote forests of Vietnam, Myanmar and Sumatra while another two potential new species are still being considered by scientists, and it seems quite possible that there are yet further species still awaiting discovery.

Fossil records suggest that the species which we in Britain are most interested in, Reeves's muntjac – also known as the Chinese muntjac –

originated during the Pleistocene epoch, some 2.5 million years ago. Early fossils have been found in China, and it is in China that our story continues. Enter John Russell Reeves (1804–1877). Like his father before him, Reeves worked for the British East India Company in Canton. Both were eminent amateur naturalists and were in turn elected Fellows of the Royal Society, and both are credited with having described new species to science. It was Reeves junior, however, who is credited with the muntjac species which bears his name.

Since he was associated with the business of exporting valuable commodities from the far east to western Europe, it is not surprising that many of the species he collected found their way to Britain, and in 1838 Reeves brought from Kwantung, southern China, to the Gardens of the London Zoological Society a pair of deer that were initially given the name *Cervus reevesi*, though this was later changed to *Muntiacus reevesi*, the name by which the species is known today. Both animals died within three months, but they were survived by a six week old fawn. There is a record of Reeves's muntjac in the private collection of the Earl of Derby at Knowsley Hall, Lancashire, in 1854, and in 1867, 1873 and 1874 there were further purchases by the Zoological Society, which in 1881 passed a female born in 1879 to the future Lord Rothschild for his collection at Tring Park, Hertfordshire. The records of that collection were destroyed during the war, but it is likely that captive muntjac were present at Tring at least for a further 20 years and escapees may well have contributed to the early population of free living muntjac in the area.

Between 1890 and 1891 Lord Herbrand Russell obtained several Indian muntjac for his collection at Cairnsmore, Dumfries and Galloway, and these were transferred to the family seat at Woburn Abbey, Bedfordshire in 1893 when Herbrand Russell succeeded his brother as 11th Duke of Bedford. This event signals an important turning point in the story of muntjac in Britain, for the 11th Duke had an abiding interest in animals and natural history and was for 37 years President of the Zoological Society. Although the deer park at Woburn had probably been established as early as 1661, it was in the late 19th and early 20th centuries that it expanded and flourished under the 11th Duke's guidance as one of the world's great collections of deer, at its peak holding 40 different species. The significance of Woburn in the deer world is not to be underestimated, for the estate and deer park have played a vital role in international deer conservation, including the saving from extinction of the Père David deer and its eventual return to China.

The first Reeves's muntjac to arrive at Woburn were six animals purchased as three separate pairs from the animal dealer William Jamrach in 1894. Their origin is not entirely clear, and they may have come from several sources, whether in China or other collections in mainland Europe such as the Jardin des Plantes in Paris. At any rate, Reeves's muntjac started breeding in the enclosures at Woburn two years after their introduction there, and although they were not particularly successful – over the first eight years just eight fawns were born – the Duke of Bedford continued to import deer both from collections such as Berlin Zoo and directly from China or Taiwan.

By 1906, 28 Reeves's muntjac had been imported to Woburn. This was far fewer than the 115 Indian muntjac which had been introduced there, and yet the Reeves's proved to be better survivors. Neither species thrived in the enclosures, perhaps because of the policy of minimal interference and a consequent lack of supplementary feeding, and in 1901, 11 Reeves's muntjac were released into the woods outside the park, where they were joined the following year by 25 Indian muntjac.

The deer park at Woburn flourished under the 11th Duke of Bedford to become the home of one of the world's great collections of deer

This parallel release of two separate muntjac species has been the cause of much confusion down the years, and for a long while it was assumed that the deer which were popping up in the surrounding countryside were either Indian muntjac or hybrids between the two species. It is now clear, however, that the Indian species did not thrive subsequent to their release and that they died out in the wild, although they may have continued to survive in the park until 1930. Certainly none existed there in 1949 when G K Whitehead surveyed the deer at Woburn.

Colonisation and Spread

As for the Reeves's muntjac, slowly and steadily they started to establish themselves. There was no culling of muntjac at Woburn at the time, but nevertheless sightings were rare in the early years. During World War 1, 'barking deer' were heard around the neighbouring village of Woburn Sands, and there are a few possible records from elsewhere in Bedfordshire and from Ashridge on the borders of Bedfordshire and Hertfordshire dating from the 1920s.

Although some of these early records were of deer that had originated from Woburn, long recognised as the principal source of Britain's naturalised population, there were other sources too. Tring Park has already been mentioned, but potentially there were more, such as the Zoological Society's collection at Whipsnade Park, which in 1928 received a pair of Reeves's muntjac from Woburn. The animals were allowed to roam free and although the records of Reeves's and Indian muntjac kept there are confused, it is evident that the Reeves's muntjac bred successfully. Furthermore, they would have had no trouble in escaping into the wider countryside through the small breaches which inevitably appeared in the surrounding fence. Ampthill House, Bedfordshire, was the site of another exotic collection during the 1930s and although it is not known whether any muntjac were kept there, Reeves's muntjac were known to occur nearby at Maulden Wood by the end of the decade.

Were muntjac to have set about colonising their new country on their own four feet from their Bedfordshire bridgehead, then it seems impossible that they could successfully have conquered the enormous range which they now occupy. Granted, the habitat across much of southern England is ideal for the species, with mostly arable farmland interspersed with mixed woodland and divided by hedgerows, but even against this background, it has been calculated that in the absence of any human interference, muntjac might be capable of spreading at a rate of 1km per year. Clearly wheels, not just feet, were involved.

Strong circumstantial evidence points to early deliberate releases on the borders of Buckinghamshire and Northamptonshire and in Warwickshire. Muntjac were seen in 1933–4 in Salcey Forest and Yardley Chase, while Rockingham Forest, 30 km to the north, was evidently colonised by 1940. Meanwhile they were present in the woods around Kineton in Warwickshire by 1941 and it is likely that many of the woods between Kineton, Coventry and Warwick held muntjac at around the same time. The suggestion is therefore that deliberate releases occurred both in Northamptonshire and Warwickshire during the early 1930s.

Other releases are much better documented. From 1947, possibly up to 1952, the 12th Duke of Bedford sought to establish free-living colonies of Reeves's muntjac, and he did this by deliberately releasing groups of four females and five males aged from 2–3 years. The deer were caught in nets at Woburn, individually crated and transported by lorry at night or in the early hours of the morning. Sites for release were personally selected by the Duke, and the deer were released one at a time by the lorry driver and his assistant. The recorded sites at which these releases were made were at Bix Bottom, Oxfordshire; near Bicester, Oxfordshire; Elveden, Suffolk; Corby, Northamptonshire; and a further unknown location in Kent.

Muntjac had been given a very significant opportunity to establish themselves across southern and eastern England and that is precisely what they did. Populations were soon rooted throughout Buckinghamshire, Northamptonshire and Oxfordshire, and across the Breckland of Norfolk and Suffolk. Only in Kent did the species fail to become established.

Unrecorded releases continued. For example, there is an eyewitness account of a muntjac, believed to have come from Bedfordshire, being released near Brandon, Suffolk, before D-Day in 1944. This is only a few miles from Elveden where a planned release was to be made some three years later. By 1953 the first sightings of muntjac had been made nearby in Thetford Forest and in 1961 a buck was killed during a game shoot on the Elveden estate. The incident obviously caused much interest amongst the Guns, who

REEVES' or CHINESE MUNTJAC *(Muntiacus reevesi)*

Reeves' (or Chinese) Muntjac, Muntiacus reevesi, male, killed on the
Elveden Estate at Elveden Gap (TL 836798, 29th January 1961).

Painting of a buck killed during a game shoot on the Elveden estate on 29 January 1961

were evidently amazed by the appearance of the strange beast which had 'nostrils' below the eyes as well as in the nose. One Gun is said to have told the gamekeeper: 'I think your dog has caught the devil!' A painting was made of the buck and this was hung in the Elveden estate museum.

Sightings of muntjac far from pre-existing populations point to further deliberate releases. One was rescued from the sea at Lowestoft, Suffolk in 1952 and two were seen at nearby Leiston, but Suffolk is a big county and these locations on the east coast are some 80km from Elveden. Were they to have spread unaided, muntjac could not possibly have covered that distance in five years, and human agency must therefore be presumed. By the late 1950s muntjac were recorded in the south and west of England, with animals reported in Berkshire (1956), Gloucestershire (1958), Avon (1959), Dorset (1962), Somerset (1966), West Sussex (1966) and Hampshire (1970).

It was by now recognised that the muntjac was widely established throughout southern England and the creatures were starting to become familiar to country people such as foresters and gamekeepers. Even so, little was known or understood about their biology, even by those best placed to observe them in the field. A commentator in *Gamekeeper and Countryside* writing in 1968 was unaware of their aseasonal breeding pattern, suggesting that they mate towards the end of winter and drop their fawns 'from late summer up to November or even December'. He even suggested the possibility that the species was at least partly carnivorous, 'for instances of the Muntjacs chasing birds, running with their heads held down low, and barking like a dog, have been seen – though they may have been merely driving the birds away for some reason, or indulging in play.'

The pattern of colonisation appears to have been one of slow growth for 10–20 years after the arrival of the species in a new area, followed by a much more rapid rate of increase once a 'critical mass' had been achieved. There does however seem to have been a significant brake applied to the growth of the muntjac population during the exceptionally severe winters of 1947 and 1963. Most of England was under snow cover from the end of January until 13 March, 1947, and during that period 70 muntjac were found dead on

The exceptionally severe winters of 1947 and 1963 caused significant muntjac mortality

rides in Hazelborough Forest, Northamptonshire. The winter of 1963 saw less snow, but the severe weather in England and Wales extended from the end of December until 6 March, with extremely low temperatures making it one of the coldest winters on record. The impact upon newly establishing muntjac populations was significant, with 33 being found dead in Salcey Forest, 10 in Yardley Chase, 20 in Hazelborough Forest and 18 in Ampthill Forest, believed to be a third of the population in the locality. Some of these animals were reported to have been killed by dogs, but there can be little doubt that this in turn was due to their weakened condition.

Reports to the British Deer Society, which held its inaugural meeting towards the end of that winter on 24 February, 1963, all suggested that muntjac had suffered a severe setback. Curiously, though, more recent cold winters have produced few reports that might suggest any significant winter-kill, although in February 1994 about half of the muntjac population in Monks Wood, Cambridgeshire, died, mainly from pneumonia after the animals were weakened by starvation.

By the 1980s muntjac had spread across central southern England and the midlands, with odd peripheral reports from Cumbria, Yorkshire, Denbighshire, Gloucestershire and Cornwall, and by the mid 1990s they had been recorded from nearly half the 10km squares in England and Wales, with only Cleveland, Durham, Greater Manchester, Merseyside, and Tyne and Wear uncolonised, though in the majority of counties the pattern was one of a sparse population overall, albeit with local concentrations of animals.

Two factors, apart of course from the availability of suitable habitat, may have assisted the spread of the species. One is the remarkable potential of female muntjac to continue to produce young throughout their adult lives. With the ability to mate and conceive within 36 hours of giving birth, a muntjac doe has a formidable reproductive capability and thus where the habitat is favourable, a few individuals can establish a new colony in a relatively short space of time. A second important factor is that muntjac occupy a near-vacant ecological niche in the British countryside and therefore have very little competition. There is little overlap with fallow deer, since muntjac are predominantly browsers and fallow mainly grazers, so the two have been able to share habitats. Clearly there must be some competition with roe deer, but in many areas into which muntjac were spreading, at least during their principal period of range expansion, roe were not present.

Above: By the 1980s, muntjac had spread across central southern England and the midlands

Left: The formidable reproductive capacity of the female muntjac has been an important factor in the successful spread of the species

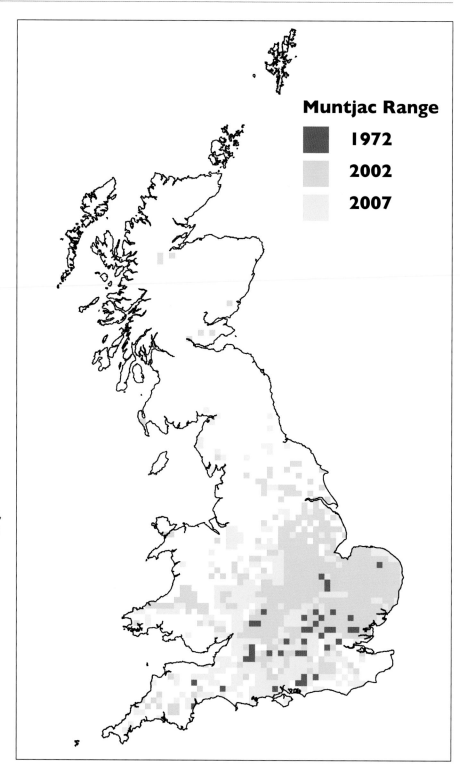

The increase in muntjac range as recorded by the British Deer Society's surveys in 1972, 2002, 2007 (Map 1) and 2011 (Map 2). Records for 10km grid squares are based on observations reported by BDS members (1972, 2002, 2007) and by BDS members and other organisations (2011). The species was considered to be present when at least one sighting was reported within the 10km square.

Map 1 shows the establishment and spread of muntjac through southern and eastern England

Muntjac Range

1972
2002
2007

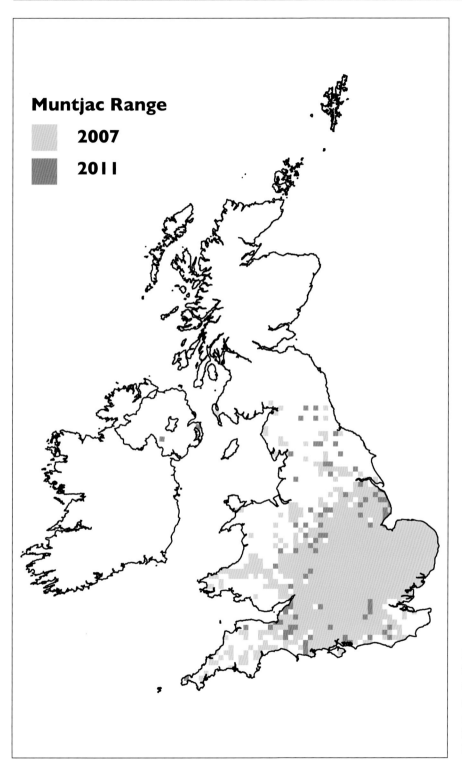

Muntjac Range

2007

2011

Map 2 illustrates the continued range expansion northwards and westwards, with new records confirmed for the first time in Northern Ireland

In the thirty years between 1972 and 2002 no other British species of deer exceeded the rate of range expansion achieved by the muntjac. As measured by its presence in 10km squares, it achieved an annual rate of increase of 8.2%, compared to 1.8% for fallow, 2.3% for roe and 2.0% for Chinese water deer. Over the following five years to 2007, which saw substantial increases in range by all species, the muntjac's rate of change increased to 11.6%, more than twice that of roe (5.2%) though less than that of fallow (12.5%) or Chinese water deer (22.2%), the latter species by then establishing itself rapidly from a small initial base.

The most recent quinquennial survey conducted by the British Deer Society in 2011 shows a continued penetration southwards, westwards and northwards from the margins of its existing range, and areas in which muntjac may now be found include parts of West Sussex, Dorset, Somerset, Derbyshire, Staffordshire, Lincolnshire, Yorkshire, Cumbria and Northumberland. So far as is known, wild muntjac are not yet present north of the Scottish border. They have, however, established themselves in Ireland. A muntjac was reported in 2008 to have been shot in the Wicklow area, and the species is now also resident in Northern Ireland.

That man is largely responsible for enabling the muntjac to expand and consolidate its position over so much of the United Kingdom is self-evident. Without the enthusiasm of those mid 19th century naturalists who shipped it from the far east, the species would never have reached these shores in the first place, but thereafter the repeated introductions to selected sites have enabled it to leapfrog its way around the country far faster than would ever have been possible were individual animals to have been left to colonise the countryside without human assistance. The reasons for such introductions and the transferring of animals from one site to another are no doubt diverse, ranging from a genuine desire by some to complement Britain's natural fauna with what was at one time seen as a rare and exotic creature, to a wish to

Involuntary translocation: this buck survived a 25 mile ride through Hertfordshire in the front bumper of a car

establish a new species for sporting purposes and even a humanitarian concern for the welfare of particular individuals. Many muntjac, for instance, are known to have been 'rescued', often from urban situations and released, perhaps after treatment for injuries, into nearby favourable habitat. Occasionally translocations are entirely involuntary, such as the instance in which a muntjac buck took a 25 mile ride through Hertfordshire after being hit by a car and becoming trapped, unbeknown to the driver, in the front bumper. The buck survived with nothing more than cuts and bruises and was released by a veterinary surgeon at Borehamwood.

Notwithstanding the help it has received from humankind, however, the muntjac has proved itself supremely adept at exploiting the habitat available to it in Britain. It has shown itself to be adaptable, bold and resilient: capable of bouncing back when faced with weather events which are unknown in its native country.

Attitudes towards introduced exotic species have changed greatly since the days of John Reeves or indeed the 11th Duke of Bedford, and today the far reaching consequences of introductions of non-native species upon natural habitats and native fauna and flora, not to mention man's own economic activities, are far better recognised than they once were. In 1997 Reeves's muntjac was added to Schedule 9 of the Wildlife and Countryside Act 1981, since when it has been an offence to release muntjac or deliberately to allow them to escape from captivity, and in 2008 the UK Government launched its Invasive Non-Native Species Framework Strategy for Great Britain. However, while preventing further release is one thing, eliminating an established population is quite another, for only two naturalised mammals have successfully been eradicated from these islands – the muskrat in 1937 and the coypu in 1987. Nobody today suggests that it might be remotely possible to eliminate the muntjac, indeed it is evident that translocations, albeit illegal ones, are still being made. How else did the species make the leap to Northern Ireland?

In little over 100 years the muntjac has grown from an exotic – even outlandish – curiosity confined in a few collections, to a widely established and commonplace species across much of England which continues to spread into new localities where it provides grief and worry to some and delight, wonder and pleasure to others. Either way, it has proved itself to be phenomenally successful, and it is hard to see how even its sternest opponent can fail at least to pay it grudging acknowledgement for that.

2 NATURAL HISTORY

Size

The Reeves's or Chinese muntjac, is Britain's smallest species of deer. A mature buck stands up to about 50cm in height, with the doe standing a couple of centimetres shorter, making a muntjac about the same size as a Labrador. Published sources indicate that the average live weight for an adult buck is reckoned to be around 14kg, with the doe around 2kg lighter, though it must be remembered that females will usually be carrying unborn young at some stage of development. Deer stalkers usually record the larder weight, that is to say the weight of the animal after gralloching and basic preparation, with the carcass still in the skin but with head and legs removed. This is reckoned to represent about 68% of live weight. A quick check of my own larder records, excluding immature animals, shows an average larder weight of 9.35kg across both sexes, which would suggest live weight of a little under 14kg, but with bigger bucks running up to 16kg on the hoof. That is a substantial size for a muntjac, although bucks of over 20kg are not unknown.

Colour and Markings

At birth, the fawn weighs a little over 1kg and appears about the size of a small hare. Its brown coat has a darker dorsal stripe and is covered with pale spots arranged in lines along its flanks. These act as an excellent camouflage when it is stationary in dense undergrowth and trying to avoid detection. After about two months the spots fade, and the adult muntjac's summer coat is an attractive chestnut brown, sleek and silky in texture. This changes in winter to a denser, thicker coat which is slightly darker and greyer in colour. In spring, animals take several weeks to moult, and in April and May they will often be found looking like a motheaten blanket as patches of the longer winter coat are shed. The underside of both sexes is a creamy white.

A doe in her sleek, chestnut brown summer coat, with her young fawn

Bucks have strongly pronounced dark V-shaped facial markings, extending from the middle of the face between the pronounced sub-orbital glands, up the fronts of the two bony ridges to the pedicles. These markings make the facial ridges very prominent and at one time led to muntjac being known as 'rib-faced deer'. Does, meanwhile, have a dark kite-shaped pattern on the forehead.

There can however be considerable variation in colour, and the winter coat sometimes appears quite a light grey. On more than one occasion when a pale muntjac has appeared in front of my high seat, partially obscured by vegetation, I have had to study it quite hard before confirming its identity for while the size, shape and general characteristics have shouted 'muntjac!' the colour has suggested something very different. Far more dramatic was the experience of a very good stalking friend of mine who on one occasion saw an animal which 'had the look of a mountain hare in its winter coat'. At first he took it to be a large cat with no tail, and it was only when the animal jumped a

The doe has a dark, kite-shaped pattern on her forehead

Above Left: In winter the coat becomes denser and thicker in texture and slightly darker and greyer in colour

Above Right: A rare leucistic muntjac photographed alongside a normal-coloured buck in his winter coat

Right: Occasionally muntjac may be found with additional white markings. This animal has extensive white markings on his hind legs and a very unusual white blaze on the forehead

single strand of barbed wire that he could clearly see that it was a very pale coloured muntjac buck. Luckily he had his rifle with him and the result was a rare leucistic muntjac. Even more luckily, he had already shot another, normal coloured buck earlier that day and was able to take a photograph of the two side by side for comparison. Muntjac are occasionally seen with unusual white markings, in particular white 'socks' on the lower legs, while a white 'blaze' to the front of the face is not unknown.

General Appearance

The tail on both sexes is about 15cm in length and is carried pointing downwards when the animal is undisturbed. When alarmed, however, it is raised vertically like a flag, showing the brilliant white underside which flashes as the muntjac bounds away, usually into the nearest heavy cover. For the stalker, the tail is a very useful indicator of the degree to which an animal has been alarmed. Sometimes a muntjac, perhaps having observed an unusual movement, will skip quickly into cover. If its tail is down, then there is a good chance that within two or three minutes it will reappear and present a potential shot. If, however, it is showing the white flag as it disappears, then the likelihood is that it will keep running until it is well clear of the potential danger.

When walking at a normal pace, the muntjac presents a rather hunched appearance, with the back rounded, the head down and the hind quarters apparently higher than the shoulders. It is usually on the move and tends not to stray far from cover, keeping close to hedges or cover strips when it is away from woodland, and feeding as it walks, hesitating only long enough to take a bite before continuing on its way. This steady walking gait will also be used when a muntjac moves across open ground, usually whilst travelling from one wood to another. When alarmed, however, muntjac have a surprising turn of speed and will gallop fast to escape from danger, especially when forced to emerge into the open, such as when they are pushed out of a drive at a game shoot.

When alarmed, a muntjac will raise its tail vertically, flashing the brilliant white underside as it runs into cover

Antlers

Adult muntjac bucks carry a pair of antlers, usually around 8-10cm in length in a mature animal. These grow from a long bony pedicle that extends well beyond the top of the skull, sometimes making the antlers appear longer than they actually are when the animal is observed at a distance. The first antlers are little more than short spikes, extending directly out of the pedicles, but successive heads will develop the longer, curved antler of the adult buck, often with a backward twist at the end. A fully mature head will have an additional pair of brow tines emerging just above the coronet. These rarely exceed about 1cm in length. On very rare occasions, multi-pointed heads have been recorded.

Most bucks shed their antlers between May and early July and re-grow them during the latter part of the summer though, as is always the case with wild animals, no rule is ever immutable and I once handled a large, mature buck with newly-shed antlers in the second week of March. In late summer, the antlers will usually be covered in velvet, a soft skin that is rich in blood vessels and which nurtures the fast-growing antler within. Antler development is, however, quite complex as a result of the fact that muntjac breed all the year round. Bucks start to develop their pedicles at about 5 months of age and then grow their first antlers four or five months after that. Subsequently, the young buck will synchronise the date at which it casts its antlers to the midsummer norm, thus an animal born in late spring will grow his first antlers towards the end of the following winter and keep them right through until midsummer the following year when he is over two years old, whereas one born in late winter may shed his first antlers at the age of only fourteen months.

In late summer, the buck's developing antlers are covered in velvet

Variation in antler shape may be less remarkable than in other deer species simply because the basic shape is less complex, but it is no less interesting to the muntjac enthusiast. The pedicles of younger bucks are longer in relation to the size of the skull, while the set of the pedicles can range from a wide v-shape to an almost parallel formation. Pedicle length reduces with successive heads, and antler shape will range from a short, thick, almost pyramidal structure to the classic curved, back-swept beam with well-defined brow points.

Tusks

Muntjac of both sexes have canine tusks. Those of the doe are vestigial and barely show below the gum. Those of the buck, however, are very pronounced. They are backward curved with, in a fully mature animal, a subtle and very beautiful outward flick. They have a razor-sharp rear edge and are used both for fraying saplings in order to mark territories, and for fighting, when they represent a fearsome weapon. Dogs are occasionally injured quite severely by muntjac bucks, as a near neighbour of mine once discovered when her cocker spaniel picked a fight with one that had ventured into her garden. The buck got by far the better of the encounter and severed an artery in the spaniel's neck. Had it not been for the quick actions of the local vet, the dog would have been lost. Tusks remain dangerous even after a buck has been shot, indeed, many is the stalker who has received post-mortem retribution from the tusks of a dead muntjac whilst gralloching or removing the head without due care and attention.

Antler development, clockwise from bottom left: Fawn at approximately 6 months of age, with pedicles just forming; under a year old, pedicles have grown; first antlers with no coronets; 3rd year buck with coronets but no clearly defined brow points; mature buck with good representative head; old buck with medal class head; post mature buck 'going back' – note short, heavy boned pedicles and brow ridges, and uneven length of antlers

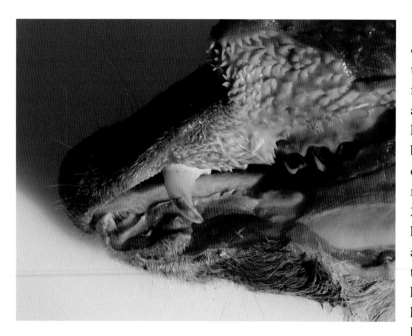

The buck's tusks have a backward curve and a sharp rear edge

The buck's tusks grow quickly. Measured around the curve of the exposed tusk from the point of emergence, a length of about 20mm will have grown by the time a buck is 14 months old. Bucks of three to five years have a mean exposed tusk length of 29mm, though this is only half of the total, for as much again remains buried in the jaw. The breakage rate, however, is very high, and a large proportion of bucks will have some damage to their tusks, if not a complete loss of one or both. In one study, just over half of 83 bucks estimated to be three to five years old had at least one broken tusk and only 39% of 58 bucks over five years old had both tusks intact. Once broken, a tusk will not re-grow. However, if it is removed from the skull and examined, it can give a good indication of the age of the buck. As the animal gets older, the open root of the tusk gradually closes. Thus a young buck has a wide open root, the walls of which are quite thin and brittle. From the age of three years the root progressively closes and after five years there is only a pinprick left.

Tusk development, left to right: Young buck with open root; three to five years with root closing; over five years, with only a pinprick left

Feeding and Behaviour

Muntjac are principally a browsing species, preferring the highly nutritious shoots, leaves and buds of shrubs, trees and climbing plants such as ivy. Bramble is a particular favourite, and muntjac may often be observed lingering along a bramble hedge, selecting and picking off the fresh young shoots. They are catholic in their tastes, however, and will consume berries, acorns and chestnuts in the autumn and the shoots, blooms and leaves of a wide variety of flowering plants during the spring and summer, notably bluebells, cowslips and oxlips. This, together with their predilection for re-growth from coppice stools, brings them into direct conflict with the management of woodland of high nature conservation importance.

Bramble is a favourite food

While their native habitat is the sub-tropical forest of south east Asia, muntjac in Britain prefer deciduous woodland, especially that in which there is a dense understorey. Thus the abundance of small, unmanaged woodlands in lowland England which provide a thick tangle of unkempt vegetation at ground level has contributed greatly to the muntjac's ability to increase both in range and population. The species is, however, able to adapt well to a wide range of wooded habitats. Managed plantations of deciduous trees, especially when densely planted, together with old hazel coppice are particularly suitable, but small, unkempt spinneys, areas of scrub, overgrown railway embankments and thick hedgerows are equally likely to hold muntjac.

They are perfectly content to coexist at close quarters with the human population, and muntjac will exploit the opportunities offered by large gardens, shrubberies, cemeteries, golf courses, roadside plantings and even the densely planted centres of large suburban roundabouts. Where a natural corridor leads into a town, then they will sometimes be found deep inside urban environments, and there are regular stories in local newspapers of muntjac being encountered in bizarre situations. One was found inside the main postal sorting office of my nearby market town not so long ago, apparently having penetrated the town along the green corridor of dense riverbank vegetation which runs along the back of the building. More serious for the muntjac is the prospect of their getting trapped in fences, railings and gates or drowning in uncovered swimming pools.

Unlike red or fallow deer, muntjac are regarded as a solitary rather than a herding species, but this description masks the complex social interplay which exists within the muntjac population. While they tend to be seen alone, there are many occasions on which two or more animals may be observed together. Sometimes this will be a buck and a doe, or equally likely an adult doe and a well-grown youngster. However, on occasions many more muntjac may be seen in each others' company. I have seen six together in a sugar beet field alongside a wood, but I have heard reliable reports of over 20 muntjac being seen together. Both bucks and does establish territories in much the same way as do roe, the bucks' territories being rather larger and overlapping the territories of several does. Territories are marked with scent from the sub-orbital glands situated in the large sockets in front of the eyes, and from the frontal glands on the forehead. These are rubbed against vegetation within or on the edge of the territory, and in particular upon saplings which a buck

This buck is marking his territory with scent from the frontal glands on his forehead

has frayed. Muntjac will also mark territories with shallow scrapes. There is no doubt that bucks will defend their territories against any rival. Sometimes this will involve a vocal challenge to the intruder from the edge of a territory, perhaps leading to a long and drawn-out barking match between two bucks, but fights are commonplace.

The principal weapon appears to be the tusks which, as we have already seen, are very sharp and purpose-made for fighting. The head and neck are the main targets and muntjac are naturally built to withstand attack in this area, with mature males having a very thick, tough skin around the nape of the neck. Even so, an old buck will usually be found to have cuts and gashes to his face, neck or flanks. On one occasion I shot a buck which had a fresh, deep

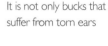

It is not only bucks that suffer from torn ears

28cm long slash to its flank that can only have been caused by the tusks of another buck. Cut or torn ears are also frequent, and that such injuries are most likely to be the result of fighting is evidenced by the fact that in one study, bucks were found to be ten times more likely than does to have torn or cut ears. If a buck breaks one or more of his tusks, then this places him at a serious disadvantage in a fight. Breakages are common

and one stalker of my acquaintance has actually found the broken point of a tusk embedded in the hock joint of a three year old buck that was obviously involved in a fight. Very occasionally I have come across bucks that have been blinded in one eye, presumably during fights, and on two occasions the bucks concerned were large, mature animals of medal quality. One I found dead and the other I shot. Equally interesting was the fact that both had broken tusks, suggesting that big old bucks of such status are prepared to stand their ground despite their obvious disadvantage.

Breeding

As is well known, muntjac are aseasonal breeders and does may mate or give birth at any time of the year. They achieve sexual maturity upon reaching a weight of around 10kg, usually at seven months of age, whereupon they come into oestrus and will mate for the first time. Thereafter follows a life of reproduction, for within 36 hours of the birth of her fawn, the doe will come into oestrus once more and be available for mating. If mating is not successfully achieved immediately, then she will continue to come into oestrus every two weeks until she is pregnant. Thus a female muntjac is pregnant for most of her adult life. Bucks will achieve sexual maturity at about nine months and remain fertile thereafter, irrespective of the various stages of the antler cycle.

The fawn is born after a 210 day gestation period and for a few days will remain quietly hidden in thick cover while the doe is feeding. Thereafter it will quickly become active and accompany its mother. In general, fawns will become independent at about two months of age, about the same time as they start to develop their adult colouration, however, in captivity they have been seen to suckle at up to 17 weeks.

Do muntjac have multiple births? That is a question which stalkers and deer watchers have been asking for many years and until quite recently there was no settled view upon the matter. However, there have now been sufficient reports of does accompanied by twin fawns, from knowledgeable and reliable stalkers, to make it certain that on rare occasions live twins may be born and survive, at least through the first weeks of life. A few photographs exist of what appear to be twins and there is even a lucky piece of video footage in which it is clear beyond reasonable doubt that the two fawns are attached to a single doe.

Fawns will be taken by badgers and foxes, which are the main cause of natural mortality in juveniles, but an adult that is close by will vigorously defend a fawn that is threatened by a predator. Once having reached adulthood a muntjac, in common with other deer species, will have no natural predators in Britain.

A rare picture of a muntjac doe with twin fawns

Communication

Another former name for the muntjac is the barking deer, and it is this bark which is one of the most distinctive features about the species. Both sexes bark, and the call is often described as similar to that of a small dog. In general that is fairly accurate, but if you listen carefully to muntjac, you will soon detect a wide variety of different notes, calls or accents, from a hoarse cough to a shrill yap. There are many muntjac in the hedgerows and spinneys around where I live, and I sometimes stand outside under the stars on a quiet night and listen to their barking. Each is different, and it seems clear to me that their voices must be as individual to other muntjac as ours are to other humans.

Muntjac bark when they are alarmed. When an animal has detected danger but has not actually confirmed its nature or location then it will stand and challenge repeatedly. This occurs, for example, when a muntjac catches the merest whiff of your scent in a very light and unsteady breeze or detects an unusual movement. The moment that danger is confirmed, it will turn and run into cover, flagging with its tail and barking repeatedly. If it is satisfied that there is a false alarm then, having stood and barked for some time, it will stop barking but remain on the alert for some minutes before finally relaxing and going about its business.

Barking is also used for social communication. Sometimes animals will bark repeatedly as they move steadily through a wood, to advertise their presence. They will also bark to mark or defend their territories, and on occasions, a single bark, repeated every 7 seconds or so, will continue for up to an hour. Listen carefully and you will hear that the note and volume will change from time to time, occasionally sounding muffled for a few barks before becoming clear again. This is an indication that an animal may be walking round in circles, the bark sounding muffled as the muntjac turns away. I have watched a muntjac buck behaving in this way during what has quite evidently been a territorial challenge with another buck.

Muntjac fawns will make a squeal or bleat when in danger, and this quickly draws the attention of any nearby adult, which may rush in vigorously to challenge the threat. It is the imitation of the fawn's note, and the reaction which it elicits from a nearby adult, that is the basis for the fascinating strategy of muntjac calling.

Some observers have heard muntjac make a chattering noise or click their teeth, though I have not been lucky enough to do so. They will also squeal when in distress, such as when caught by a dog.

One autumn night I was just about to go to bed when I heard an ear-piercing shriek that seemed to come from just a few metres outside the bedroom window. At first it sounded to me like one of the female tawny owls which we sometimes get in the trees outside the front of the house, and it was only after I had opened the window and listened for a short while to the repeated shriek that my wife correctly identified the sound as being the distress call of a muntjac. We had that afternoon moved our flock of sheep and a muntjac buck, obviously using his familiar route across the meadow, had blundered into the electric sheep netting and got himself entangled. Every couple of seconds he was getting a belt from the battery-powered energizer and the call was his response. It did not take us more than a few minutes to run downstairs, pull on our boots, switch off the power and release the buck, which ran off into the night apparently none the worse for his ordeal. The sheep appeared totally unconcerned by the performance, but it provided us with a warning to

Plastic marker tape may discourage muntjac from attempting to push through sheep netting

be careful when using electric sheep netting close to regular muntjac runs. If such use is unavoidable, then there may be benefit in making the netting more visible to approaching deer by using plastic marker tape.

Signs

If you do not see the actual animal itself, then the most obvious sign that a muntjac has been about are its footprints or slots. These are considerably smaller than those of any other deer species, though they could possibly be

Muntjac slot mark

confused with those of an immature Chinese water deer in places where both species are present. They are quite dainty and shaped a little like a teardrop. When a muntjac is walking at its normal pace, then the slot marks will form a single line and with experience it is possible to get some idea of the size and weight of the animal that made them. Regular paths through woodland, exits through the woodland perimeter or

Left: Muntjac are using the 'tramlines' through this sugar beet field to move back and forth from the woodland that can be seen on the horizon

Middle: This crossing point over a stream is well-marked with muntjac slots

Right: A muntjac scrape in early spring

favourite crossing places over ditches will often carry quantities of fresh slot marks and the presence of these marks represent a good rule-of-thumb means of gauging population levels.

Of course the presence of slot marks and the length of time that they remain identifiable as such are directly related to the nature of the soil and its softness. Sandy soil is good at revealing the passage of deer, but slot marks will not last for long. Clay, on the other hand, will only take an impression when the soil is wet, but when it does so, the impression may remain for many days or weeks, depending of course on subsequent rainfall. It is thus worth getting to know the rate at which slot marks decay on the ground where you regularly hunt or observe muntjac. Really fresh slot marks will appear absolutely crisp, perhaps even with the impression of hair if the mark is in wet clay. Thereafter they will lose definition, particularly after a shower or a longer period of rain, until eventually they are undistinguishable. If you walk a piece of ground regularly, then it is not difficult to get some idea of when fresh slot marks were made. Alternatively, if the marks are within another impression, say the tyre marks of a tractor or 4x4, and you know when the vehicle was present, then the time at which the slot mark was made is narrowed down considerably.

In summer when the ground is drier and the grass is high, it is much harder to see slot marks. However, you can still spot tunnels in vegetation which have been used by muntjac, or the places where they have pushed under

Saplings frayed by (left) muntjac and (right) roe. Note the difference in the height at which the bark has been damaged.

or through rabbit fences. It is also possible to spot trees or shrubs that have been frayed by muntjac. Usually a young sapling will be chosen, and the bark will be rubbed off between 15cm and 30cm above ground level, significantly lower than the mark made by a fraying roebuck.

Regular paths may occasionally be found across open ground

Dung pellets may be found, often along regular trails or at feeding points. The pellets are very dark brown or black, slightly elongated and glossy in appearance when fresh. They can easily be confused with those of roe deer. Pellets are usually in small clumps, and trials with captive muntjac suggest a defecation rate of seven pellet groups per day, each group ranging from 20 to 120 pellets. Scrapes may also be found in woodland.

Fresh droppings

Diurnal Activity

Like other deer species, muntjac are most frequently active around dawn and dusk, but within those broad parameters a range of interesting detail has been detected, most especially through research involving the use of camera traps at Monks Wood and Woodwalton Fen National Nature Reserves. In areas not subject to stalking, there were peaks of activity during the period three hours before dusk and two hours thereafter, with much lower peaks of activity at dawn, but with activity increasing in the first few hours after sunrise. Activity at night was relatively low. Where regular stalking occurred, the number of observations during the period before dusk decreased significantly and the amount of night-time activity increased.

The period of activity in the couple of hours after sunrise will be familiar to many regular stalkers, who often report seeing muntjac on the move in and around woodland long after other deer species have sought daytime refuge in dense cover. But for those stalkers who prefer to hunt at dawn rather than dusk, the data does offer the interesting suggestion that evening sessions might on balance be more fruitful.

Slot Mark Decay

Slot marks are surprisingly persistent in heavy soil, but they eventually decay and disappear over time and following the precipitation of rain or snow. This sequence of photographs shows the decay of a slot mark in the clay soil of an arable field margin which is regularly used by muntjac. The total precipitation since the slot mark appeared has been obtained from the farm's daily rainfall records.

1.

2.

3.

4.

5.

6.

1. February 9
The slot mark in wet clay is less than 24 hours old

2. February 10
Days passed: 1,
total precipitation 0.5mm. There is little change

3. February 11
Days passed: 2,
total precipitation 3mm. Snow has fallen and the leading edge of the footprint is starting to collapse

4. February 16
Days passed: 7,
total precipitation 12mm. The central ridge between the two cleave prints is no longer visible

5. March 13
Days passed: 31,
total precipitation 67.5mm. A month has passed with several days of heavy rain and the footprint is starting to become indistinguishable

6. March 26
Days passed: 44,
total precipitation 95mm. The footprint is no longer distinguishable, but another fresh print has appeared just in front of it

3 MUNTJAC AND MAN

For a species which owes its presence in the British Isles to man's intervention, the muntjac is capable of raising strong emotions amongst a wide range of people. While of course there are many visitors to the countryside who enjoy seeing muntjac on family walks or picnics in the forest, land managers who encounter them in the course of their work very often harbour far more negative views. Indeed, to many the muntjac is seen as nothing more than vermin. Curiously, that is particularly the case amongst those who have the least direct experience of the species. In Ireland, where muntjac have been recorded but are not by any means widespread, they have been branded as 'Ireland's most unwanted invasive species' and blamed for destroying forest understorey and even for propagating other non-native species such as rhododendron. In Scotland, where muntjac have yet to establish themselves, they are regarded with equal venom. Even Scottish deer stalkers can react strongly to the prospect of their settling north of the border, and one roe stalker writing in the British Deer Society journal *Deer* has likened them to the grey squirrel, the advance of which has caused the eradication of the native red squirrel throughout much of Britain. This is somewhat unfair to the muntjac, which is capable of coexisting quite comfortably with other deer species. Even so, muntjac, in common with other deer, do impact on natural biodiversity and man's use of the countryside in a number of ways.

Agriculture

It has to be said that in comparison with larger species such as red and fallow deer, muntjac have little impact on arable agriculture. Being by choice browsers rather than grazers, they do not pose a major threat to growing crops. Group size and the size of individual animals are also very significant here. Unlike fallow and red, muntjac do not form large and very visible herds, and of course being much smaller animals they cannot consume as much vegetation in a sitting as their larger cousins. Whereas a herd of fallow can

Muntjac do not present a significant threat to arable or livestock farming

exact significant grazing damage upon a field of cereals or oilseed rape, the effect of a few individual muntjac on an arable field is likely to be minimal.

A further problem faced by farmers with fallow or red deer on their land is the trampling or lodging effect of large numbers of deer lying down in pre-harvest cereal crops. Again, this is not an issue with muntjac, although their tracks and paths through cereal fields in the weeks before harvest may be all too conspicuous to the arable farmer.

Less obvious, though potentially of much more significance, is the possibility that deer, including muntjac, may host and then transmit diseases to farm livestock. This is a threat which has only recently started to be investigated. Bovine tuberculosis (bTB) is of massive economic importance to the dairy industry and has of course generated stark conflict between town and country insofar as to remove the threat of infection, badger culling has been given Government support. Yet all UK deer species can be infected by bTB. Prevalence within the national wild deer herd is less than 1% but there are known to be persistent hotspots amongst concentrations of deer – mostly fallow – associated with deer parks. Likewise more than 50% of deer in some parks are carrying Johne's disease, and there is a growing concern amongst livestock farmers that wild deer may be a reservoir of this too.

Neither in the case of bTB nor Johne's is there any significant evidence that muntjac, as opposed to fallow and red deer, are a problem, and where another newly established disease, Schmallenberg virus (SBV), is concerned, it would appear that muntjac again are not guilty. Results from 66 blood samples collected in 2012 from wild deer in East Anglia, where SBV is widespread, showed that while 70% of red deer samples and 62% of fallow deer samples were positive, there were no positive results for any of the roe or muntjac samples tested.

Forestry

Foresters have much more reason than farmers to be concerned about muntjac. Their tendency is, as we have seen, to browse rather than to graze, and therefore the tender shoots of newly establishing trees are at risk. One estate on which I have stalked for a number of years specialises in growing high quality oak for the timber trade. Seedlings are sourced from continental Europe, where the strongest and straightest growing genotypes may be found, and these are planted in closely spaced stands which, after 10–15 years form dense blocks of cover at ground level, making for perfect muntjac habitat. Not only do muntjac nip off the growing shoots of the young trees and cause fraying damage to small saplings, but they can also cause severe damage to the rabbit fencing with which the young plantations are enclosed, forcing their way under or through the wire and thereby allowing access by rabbits and hares. Muntjac can of course be excluded by means of deer fencing, but even then, I have on occasions seen deer fences erected to exclude red and fallow, but in which the lowest wires are sufficiently far apart to admit a determined muntjac. If it is known that muntjac are present in woodland – or are soon likely to be present – then this must be factored into any decisions related to the design of deer fencing.

Where muntjac are present, deer fencing should be designed to exclude them. This fence in a Suffolk woodland was built to prevent damage by red and fallow deer, but will easily admit muntjac

Conservation

A parallel situation to commercial forestry is that of conservation woodland where the principal objective is to allow regeneration of native trees through coppicing. This involves the rotational cutting to ground level of trees such as hazel or ash and allowing the stools to regenerate by sending up new shoots that will ideally allow the woodland to be managed in a long-term cycle of production. Periodic coppicing permits light to flood onto the woodland floor and with it there comes a surge both in the regrowth from coppiced stools and in the growth of flowering plants and shrubs of all sorts. Unfortunately muntjac, along with other deer species, will home in on the newly regenerating stools and nip off the shoots, while the rapid development of dense ground cover provides them with shelter and security. If the browsing is sufficiently severe, then over time it can kill the coppice stool altogether, which is of huge concern in ancient woodlands where individual stools may be several hundred years old. In studies in the early 1990s at Monks Wood National Nature Reserve, a 157 hectare ancient woodland in Cambridgeshire, few hazel stems in new coppice exceeded one metre because of browsing. Likewise, browsing, principally by muntjac, restricted the regeneration of young ash trees. The situation was dramatically reversed with the introduction of muntjac culling in 1998.

Destruction of shrubs and flowering plants by muntjac can, in high conservation value woodland, be of even greater significance. Bluebell woods are regarded as particularly important conservation assets and of course they are greatly loved by human visitors when the bluebells are at their peak in

Before and after, at Holme Fen, Cambridgeshire. The first photograph taken in 2006 shows bramble die-back and an impoverished fern community. The second photograph shows the recovery five years later in 2011, after the management of muntjac

Damage to bluebell leaves
reduces plant vigour and
may ultimately prevent
plants from flowering

May. But bluebells are also greatly loved by muntjac, which eat the emerging leaves in February and March and then nip off the flowering stems when they start to appear. Loss of the bluebell flowers is of course immediately visible to the human visitor, but it is the loss of the leaves that is of longer-term consequence, as this reduces the vigour of the plant, which produces smaller leaves and stems in subsequent years and which may ultimately cease flowering altogether. Other important wild flowers may suffer damage in the same way. Muntjac have a liking for orchids when these appear in the spring, and muntjac browsing has been implicated in the loss of oxlips in some woodlands in Essex.

Reduction or loss of the lower shrubby layer in woodlands through browsing by deer, muntjac in particular, is believed to be one of the causes behind the decline in one of our most loved woodland bird species, the nightingale. When the steady reduction in the number of breeding nightingales was investigated in Bradfield Woods, Suffolk, it was found that the dense understorey of bramble, honeysuckle and dog rose, important as a nesting and feeding habitat for nightingales and other woodland birds, was being lost as a result of browsing by deer. When plots within the woodland were fenced to exclude deer, it was found that the density of nightingale territories in deer-free areas was 15 times greater than in the plots to which deer had access. Across Bradfield Woods as a whole, it was found that nightingales spent 69% of their time in the 6% of the woodland from which deer had been excluded.

Oxlip browsed by muntjac

It is important to stress that this research does not make the muntjac a nightingale murderer, as has been implied by some. There are far bigger forces at work that are likely to have affected nightingale populations across the bird's huge migration range, but at the individual site level, deer browsing may well have had some effect on woodland bird populations.

Damage by deer is of major concern both to Natural England and to conservation bodies such as the RSPB and the Wildlife Trusts which own and manage woodland reserves, and it is often the cause of woodland SSSIs coming into unfavourable condition. On the other hand, where proper management of deer is carried out, rapid improvement in habitat quality can be achieved. Where several deer species are present within a woodland environment it may be difficult to establish which species is principally responsible for habitat degradation, but there is no doubt that the presence of a significant muntjac population within a woodland is likely to result in a reduction in both flowering plants and the shrubby understorey on the woodland floor. This damage may be reversed either by fencing or the introduction of muntjac control by stalking.

Gardens

When destruction of vegetation moves from the woodland wilderness into the carefully manicured surroundings of the herbaceous border or vegetable plot, then attitudes harden considerably. Damage to gardens is particularly likely where the surrounding ground provides cover for high muntjac densities but furnishes them with limited sources of food. Where damage occurs regularly, keen gardeners find the destruction of precious ornamental shrubs, fruit, flowers and vegetables infuriating. Prized roses are a favoured target and in

A raised bed failed to keep these Brussels sprouts out of the reach of muntjac

my own garden, muntjac have shown a particular liking for impatiens or busy lizzies to the extent that we no longer bother planting them. The Brussels sprouts in our raised vegetable beds and the fruit trees in our orchard have also suffered muntjac damage. Many of those who buy muntjac venison from me are gardeners, and some of them derive a considerable degree of satisfaction from the prospect of eating the creatures which have caused so much destruction in their own gardens.

Vulnerable vegetables such as beans, lettuces and courgettes can sometimes be protected with netting, cloches or chicken wire, but any covering of this sort is invariably unsightly

This doe enjoys a tasty meal from an apple tree. Any apples within reach of muntjac will be eagerly taken

and is therefore inappropriate in flower beds. Thus there is not much that can be done about damage to bedding plants or ornamentals without deer fencing the entire garden. Larger grounds with ornamental shrubberies backing on to 'wilderness' areas of nettle and unmanaged woodland provide a perfect habitat for muntjac. However, these larger and more secluded gardens sometimes offer greater opportunity for management by shooting, which is ultimately the only reliable way to deal with a troublesome muntjac. In my experience, once an individual muntjac develops a taste for the vegetables or ornamentals within a garden which offers the combination of accessibility and adjacent secure cover, then that individual will continue to return.

There are of course many people who enjoy having muntjac in the garden and who derive much pleasure from the ability to watch deer at such close quarters, especially where it is possible to recognise an individual animal or where a doe pays regular visits with her fawn. Personally, I regard it as something of a privilege to have deer living so close to me. Usually I give muntjac the benefit of the doubt and it is only when serious damage starts to occur that I take action by setting up a portable high seat and sitting out for the culprit. However, one attitude survey showed that more people were displeased at having muntjac in the garden than were pleased, so I suspect that I may be in the minority.

Gamekeeping

Gamekeepers are another group of people with cause to dislike muntjac. Just as they can force their way under or through rabbit fencing, so muntjac are equally capable of forcing their way into release pens, causing damage which provides free admittance to far less welcome pests such as foxes. Like other deer, they take expensive grain from feed rides and pheasant feeders and do not endear themselves to gamekeepers by doing so. Muntjac are quite capable of trashing a conventional feeder spring, though a feeder with a deer guard attached is less vulnerable, and muntjac will usually be unable to push a feeder over in the same way that larger species of deer might.

A further problem for gamekeepers occurs on shoot days, and especially on partridge drives when a muntjac runs forwards through the game cover crops at the crucial moment when birds are about to flush. In this situation, instead of being able to control the rate at which game lifts forwards over the Guns, the keeper is faced with a huge and unmanageable flush that sends the birds over in a single cloud that effectively ruins the drive. It is disappointing for the Guns and hugely frustrating for the keeper. Of course it is not only muntjac which cause this problem; any other small deer or indeed a fox is equally capable of doing so. But the risk of disruption to an important and carefully planned drive on a big let day certainly does not endear the muntjac to most gamekeepers.

Road Traffic Accidents

Which motorist who drives regularly in the midlands or the south east has not seen a dead muntjac at the side of the carriageway? Muntjac are involved in a large proportion of the 60,000 deer–vehicle collisions estimated to occur on the roads of England every year. Hitting a 20kg muntjac may not have the same effect on a motor vehicle and its occupants as ploughing into an

80kg fallow or a 150kg red stag, but considerable damage may be caused nonetheless. I still have the registration plate of a car which hit a muntjac outside the entrance to my property. Although his car shed various bits of plastic in the road, including the registration plate, the driver did not stop, and I was left with the task of dispatching the injured victim after the distressed lady driver in the car behind knocked on my door to say that there was a baby deer lying in the road screaming.

Right: Muntjac are involved in a large proportion of the 60,000 deer–vehicle collisions estimated to occur on the roads of England every year

Bottom Left: This buck suffered serious injury as a result of collision with a motor car

Bottom Right: The injury to the near hind leg of this buck, probably as a result of a road traffic accident, had healed well, though in late winter the animal was in poor condition when it was culled

Even more dangerous than hitting a deer is the natural reaction of a driver to swerve when an animal is spotted in the path of a vehicle, usually at night or in the poor light of dawn or dusk, resulting in a head-on collision with another vehicle travelling in the opposite direction or impact with some solid object at the roadside. There are known to be each year about 20 deaths caused by deer–vehicle collisions, but how many additional unexplained fatalities resulting from vehicles hitting roadside trees are caused by drivers swerving to avoid deer? It is a question to which nobody knows the answer, but when one of these unexplained fatalities occurred near to where I live in Suffolk, I couldn't help but wonder if the cause of a car ploughing headlong into a roadside oak tree had not been a deer running out of woodland at the side of the carriageway.

Fatalities aside, collisions with muntjac not only cause very obvious distress and trauma to drivers but they also represent a serious welfare issue to the deer themselves. Sometimes the deer is killed outright, but many more are injured to a greater or lesser extent. Impact with a fast moving vehicle causes massive trauma. I have occasionally examined road casualty muntjac and found bones and organs throughout the body to be shattered, even though the marks on the skin would suggest only a glancing blow. But muntjac are resilient creatures, and if they have enough strength to make the roadside verge and escape into cover then they will do so.

I have occasionally shot animals which have clearly suffered severe trauma, where it is most likely that the cause has been a road traffic accident. The most memorable case was a buck which had its near hind leg severed below the hock joint. This injury had healed remarkably well, and the buck was clearly able to get about well on three legs, but was in a terrible condition.

The injuries to that buck only serve to illustrate the serious effect of road traffic accidents upon the welfare of muntjac. The motor car may in 21st century Britain have replaced the lynx, wolf and brown bear as the main 'predator' of deer, but unlike those natural hunters it has no interest in following up and dispatching the wounded and injured. Deer that are not killed outright are thus left to escape and recover as best they can, and however badly the muntjac may be thought of, these little deer certainly do not deserve a lingering death in such circumstances.

Abuse by Man

It is one of the harsh facts of man's inter-relationships with animals that a creature which is not valued is subject to abuse. Sporting hunters invariably have a high regard for the quarry which they pursue, and established game species that have close seasons which afford protection during breeding periods or other stages of the annual cycle, are treated with respect. Such creatures have a value; usually one which may be rendered in hard cash by those who derive pleasure from their pursuit. Fair and appropriate means are used to kill or take them, their hunting is ethically managed in a sustainable way to ensure the long-term survival of the species and even after death they are afforded a degree of honour. In Continental Europe, a pine frond or other sprig of greenery is placed in the mouths of dead deer or wild boar to represent 'the last bite', they are laid out in rows at the end of a hunt and fanfares may be blown above them on hunting horns.

Those species that are regarded merely as pests or vermin are not afforded anything like the same degree of respect. Any available means is used to effect their destruction, and even where the law prescribes which methods may or may not be used for their control, liberties are taken that would certainly not be acceptable in a sporting context. Foxes, which enjoyed a considerable degree of respect and protection when foxhunting was a lawfully accepted sport, are now treated much more generally as vermin. They are shot – or shot at – with unsuitable weapons and at excessive ranges and I doubt that many of those which are injured or wounded in such circumstances are ever followed up and humanely dispatched.

I am often told by those who dislike or despise muntjac that they are ugly. Beauty is of course in the eye of the beholder, and whilst they may not have the grace of roe deer, I do not find muntjac unattractive. But the strongly held view that their very appearance is in some way bizarre or objectionable is the clearest indication that muntjac are considered by many to be unwelcome.

The fact that the muntjac is a non-native species that is widely seen as a mere pest or a nuisance leads inevitably to its mistreatment. The Regulatory Reform Order which in 2007 extended the range of firearms with which it is legal to shoot muntjac placed them lawfully in the sights of pest controllers using .22 centrefire foxing rifles. It did not of course extend the hours in which deer may be shot. Night shooting licences are only granted by Natural England in exceptional circumstances, and one can only wonder at the number of muntjac which are illegally taken during the hours of darkness with the aid of a lamp or a night vision riflescope.

Shotguns are of equally dubious legality. It is of course legal in some circumstances to use a shotgun to kill deer, and there is no doubt that in the correct hands a shotgun using the appropriate load of AAA at up to 25 metres is devastating. But how many of those who take a shotgun to a muntjac pay any heed to the law, let alone the niceties of range estimation? Few, I suspect, judging from the missiles which, over the years, I have extracted from the muntjac I have shot. Occasionally it is BB, which may be appropriate for fox but which is nonetheless illegal for deer, but more usually it is number 6 shot which is of course both unlawful and entirely unsuitable for a robust, medium sized, thick-skinned mammal like a muntjac.

It was the cruelty of the shotgun drives that were once used to kill roe deer which became one of the driving forces behind the Deer Act 1963 that gave protection to deer in England and Wales and lifted their status from vermin to that of game animals. Organised roe drives in late winter were not uncommon at the time. Roe were shot with shotguns and unsuitable cartridges at excessive ranges, and it was widely accepted that for every deer that was killed, another limped away to die a miserable death in thick cover.

Rumours persist of muntjac drives, though I believe it is more likely that most of the shots taken at muntjac with shotguns are not fired during the course of organised drives but at animals seen by gamekeepers and pest controllers who are moving about the woods in the course of their duties. Most such individuals are perfectly sensible people who are well aware of the capabilities of a shotgun. It therefore baffles me to think that they continue to shoot at these tough little creatures with no real hope of killing them, but in such a way that the animals run away wounded. On one buck which I shot, the whole of the face was blistered and scabby, with the hair and skin flaking away from the front of the skull, the scabs being the result of subcutaneous oedema following the discharge of a shotgun loaded with number 6 shot. I picked three pellets from beneath the skin. A fourth had penetrated the front of the skull and lodged there. The shot must have been taken front on, but miraculously the eyes had not been injured.

This was a tough old buck. I shot it from a high seat through the chest with a 150 grain .308 bullet, and the buck still ran 20 metres across a ride,

A charge of no. 6 shot to the head from a shotgun caused severe bruising to this old buck. The injury healed, though the skin was scabby and flaking when the animal was killed with a rifle bullet. Three pellets were picked from beneath the skin. A fourth lodged in the front of the skull and may be seen towards the bottom of the prepared trophy

crashed into a hazel tree, went down, got up again, turned through 180 degrees and ran another 30 metres before it finally expired. How anyone might have thought that an ounce and an eighth of number 6 from maybe 35 metres would effect a humane kill, I cannot fathom.

A further abuse which is known to take place is the coursing of muntjac with dogs. Clearly this activity is one which makes not even the smallest pretence of legality, but it is unfortunately quite widespread. As muntjac continue their range expansion across northern and western England, the fact that isolated populations of animals continue to appear is a clear indication that they are being transported by human agency, and such purely anecdotal reports as do exist suggest that the provision of quarry for coursing is one of the reasons for which these animals have been moved to new locations.

All deer require management by man, for the simple reason that in the British Isles they have no natural predators and their populations must be controlled if they are not to come into conflict with a range of land uses and activities in the countryside. Muntjac are an exotic introduction which has proved to be phenomenally successful and a significant annual cull must therefore be taken. Some deer managers suggest that the cull taken at the geographical edges of their present range should be particularly hard, in order to prevent the continued spread of the species. Whether it is possible to curb range extension I very much doubt, but one thing is self-evident: where management is undertaken, then it must be undertaken lawfully and in a way which avoids unnecessary suffering. Firm, diligent management does not equate with unethical management.

There is a widely held consensus that muntjac are 'a bad thing', but while many may hate or despise them, that is no reason to abuse the species. And of course antipathy towards muntjac by those who own or manage land opens up opportunities for deer managers who are keen to assist with responsible culling, opportunities which can provide a great deal of enjoyment from the challenges they offer.

4 STALKING PRACTICALITIES

Rifles

It was more than half a century ago that the first Deer Act elevated the status of deer in England and Wales to that of game animals. Before the Act's introduction the smaller species of deer in particular had been looked upon as little more than vermin. However, growing disquiet about the cruelty of the shotgun drives that were widely held in late winter to kill roe, coupled with new and enlightened attitudes to deer management that had been imported from continental Europe, set in train a welcome change in attitude towards deer. A new sport, that of stalking deer in the woodlands of lowland Britain, was being born, and the Deer Act 1963 established the framework in which it could develop and thrive. Among other things, it set a minimum calibre of .240 inches for rifles that could lawfully be used to shoot deer.

Though already becoming widespread in parts of southern England, the muntjac was by no means common in 1963, and the species did not figure highly in the discussions which framed the schedule of firearms regarded as suitable for killing deer. That situation changed in the early years of the present century and in 2003 a Government consultation was published which noted the increase in muntjac numbers that had taken place since the original establishment of the firearms provisions in the Deer Act and pointed out that 'the existing requirement to use the same calibres for a 9–18kg muntjac as may be used for a 150kg red deer, simply because they are both "deer", is illogical.' It made the case in favour of the use of .22 centrefire calibres for shooting both muntjac and Chinese water deer, arguing that the smaller round was no less humane and that it could be both safer and more discreet in some circumstances, such as the control of muntjac in urban and suburban situations.

A further four years elapsed before these views were translated into legislation but in 2007 the law was changed. Thus a deer stalker may today use for shooting muntjac in England and Wales:

(a)   a rifle having a calibre of not less than .220 inches and a muzzle energy of not less than 1,356 joules (1,000 foot pounds), and

(b)   a soft-nosed or hollow-nosed bullet weighing not less than 3.24 grammes (50 grains).

In practice this allows the use of a number of common .22 centrefire rounds including the .222 Rem, 5.56/.223 Rem, .22-250 Rem and .220 Swift, in addition to the larger calibres of .243 Win and above which are more normally associated with deer stalking. The .22 centrefires definitely have their very strong supporters, particularly amongst those who regularly use them for fox control, and one of the arguments advanced in their favour back at the turn of the present century was that gamekeepers who used them for foxing would be able to shoot muntjac with the same rifle and thus potentially increase the national cull. There is no doubt that with their flat trajectory and low recoil they are both accurate and very comfortable to shoot. They do have their detractors, however, who argue that high velocity .22 centrefire cartridges, when used with rapidly-fragmenting 'varmint' bullets, do not provide adequate penetration to deliver the energy required to dispatch a muntjac humanely. As anyone who has skinned one will confirm, a muntjac's skin is considerably thicker than that of a fox or even a roe deer. They are tough animals, and with the smaller calibres, the selection of a strongly constructed, slowly expanding bullet is vital.

The clincher for me, though, is that with a .22 centrefire in your hands, the only deer you may lawfully shoot is a muntjac or a Chinese water deer. On all the ground which I stalk regularly, I can potentially encounter a variety of species, and it would be both frustrating and indeed pointless were I to be at large in the woods with a .22 centrefire and have to decline the opportunity of taking a fallow or even a roe. For many years I have generally used a .308 for all species from autumn through to spring during which period I regularly encounter fallow and occasionally red deer, and a .243 with a 100 grain bullet after the end of April when muntjac is my sole quarry. In recent seasons, though, I have found myself picking up the .243 with increasing frequency throughout the winter. It is a pleasant round to shoot, it shoots relatively flat out to normal deer stalking ranges and it is sufficiently recoil-free to enable the hunter consistently to watch the reaction to shot through his riflescope.

Furthermore the .243, the most popular calibre among UK stalkers, offers a wide choice of bullet weights up to 105 grains, while ammunition is universally obtainable. There is not a self-respecting gunshop which cannot offer a box of .243 cartridges off the shelf in 100 grains or some other appropriate bullet weight, quite often in two or three different brands. No wonder the .243 is, according to a BASC survey, nearly five times as popular as its nearest rival for use against muntjac.

Let us not dismiss the larger calibres though. Some people speak darkly of excessive carcass damage, but I have rarely encountered this problem when chest shooting muntjac with my .308. You may perhaps have to put aside some of the shoulder meat to feed to the dog, but remember that even a neck shot taken with a .243 can discolour the front end of the fillets. Of course a small animal like a muntjac which is badly shot with any centrefire rifle will require the removal of some damaged venison, but humane shooting and deer welfare should in the final event trump any economic or butchery considerations. On balance, my preference when selecting a rifle that will predominantly be used to shoot muntjac would be to opt for the .243, while if there is a substantial proportion of larger species to be shot – and especially forest reds – then to 'go large' and not to worry about very occasional carcass damage from a misplaced round.

A rifle for muntjac should ideally be light, tactile, compact and handy. When shooting in and around woodland a short barrel is a real advantage, as it is much easier to carry without snagging in low-hanging foliage and undergrowth. Any loss of downrange accuracy is of little consequence, since most shots at muntjac are taken inside 70 metres, and many much closer than that. Very rarely indeed would I elect to take a shot at muntjac at 200 metres, so the increased holdover required when using a short barrel at long range is in most cases irrelevant. A short barrel also makes it much easier to lift a rifle onto your stalking sticks. It causes less movement and the manoeuvre, which often has to be performed in just a couple of seconds and perhaps within sight of the quarry, creates much less potential disturbance if you do not have several extra inches of barrel to cope with.

Choice between a traditional walnut stock, wood laminate and ABS plastic is purely a personal one, for all are sufficiently stable for the job in hand and as we have already observed, squeezing the last fraction of a millimetre of accuracy out of a rifle really is not an issue when quarry shooting at under 100 metres. I use both wood and plastic equally happily, though while the latter has a distinct advantage in wet, muddy conditions, I find the design of most plastic stocks rather clumsy. A finely made and ergonomically designed stock, whether in laminate or walnut, makes a big difference to a rifle for woodland work.

Shooting Supports

I do not use a bipod when muntjacking in the woods. Bipods are hugely valuable when stalking red deer on the open hill, and a number of my roe stalking friends use them when shooting over open farmland. However, the number of muntjac I shoot from a prone position is very small indeed, and

The overwhelming majority of shots at muntjac taken whilst stalking on foot will be from the standing position, off sticks

then it is usually a case of getting down, crawling a metre or two and taking the shot quickly before the animal walks into cover. Rarely is there the opportunity to observe an animal for an extended period and set the rifle up for a prone shot as one might do on the hill. On the contrary, most muntjac are shot off sticks or from a high seat where a bipod is nothing more than a hindrance.

Stalking sticks, on the other hand, are essential. The overwhelming majority of shots at muntjac taken whilst stalking on foot will be from the standing position, so it is essential to be able to take a steady shot off a rest whilst standing exactly where you are when you spot your quarry, without having to search for a tree to lean against that may or may not afford a clear view of the target. Any shot will generally have to be taken quickly at a quarry which is either on the move or stationary for maybe a second or less, and the deciding factor when selecting stalking sticks is the speed with which they can be deployed. My preference has always been for a pair of hazel sticks measuring the same height as myself and whipped together so that they can be opened to form a 'vee' in which the rifle is placed. I have two pairs of sticks and both of them have accounted for a great many muntjac. Of course there are many proprietory stalking sticks in bipod, tripod and even quad configurations. In my experience, the more complex they are, the longer they take to set up and in muntjac stalking, where fractions of a second count, this is a drawback.

Sound Moderators

We in Britain are lucky enough to be able to use sound moderators for our hunting. Most of those who stalk muntjac do so, and with good reason: they make using a centrefire rifle in the relatively densely-settled countryside of southern England much more discreet and acceptable, and they prevent the stalker from being temporarily blinded by the muzzle flash of a shot taken in low light. But far more importantly, they protect the stalker's hearing, enabling him to hunt without the need for additional hearing protection and thus allowing him to deploy the full complement of senses which he still retains. I hate having to take my moderators off when travelling overseas to those benighted countries in which they are still prohibited, quite apart from the irritation of having to re-zero the rifle twice – once when removing the moderator for overseas hunting and then again when replacing it upon resuming normal operations in the UK.

Sound moderator technology has advanced rapidly in recent years. These titanium moderators are far lighter and less cumbersome than their steel predecessors and are maintenance free. Two .243 cartridges are shown alongside for scale

It must be said that from the perspective of handiness and manoeuvreability, the sound moderator is a disadvantage. Unfortunately all moderators increase barrel length, even those types which partially sleeve over the barrel. Their weight and bulk also adversely affect the handling and balance of the rifle, and this was an issue to which I paid considerable attention when I first started to use moderators. After discussing the matter with two very experienced riflesmiths, I had four inches taken off the barrel of my .243. Even then, I found the first generation of steel moderators heavy and cumbersome. In recent years, however, I have turned to the newer generation of titanium moderators. These are barely larger than a cigar tube and far lighter in weight than steel moderators. Unlike steel, titanium is totally maintenance free, and these products really do work.

A simple experiment in which a sound level meter was held close to my right ear by a friendly sound engineer as I fired a series of test rounds both with and without a moderator, confirmed that at the place where it is most important, namely at the ear of the shooter, the noise was attenuated by about three quarters when one of my Quicksilver titanium moderators was fitted. That was true for both my full bore stalking rifles in .243 and .308.

Accessories

My hunting philosophy is to keep things as simple and uncomplicated as possible. I have friends who love gadgetry and who will carry all manner of the latest gizmos about their person when out stalking. I have tried a lot of them, and occasionally some piece of new kit comes to the market which is genuinely helpful. However, so far as I am concerned in most cases, less is more. Alongside my rifle, a full spare magazine and my stalking sticks, I carry two knives. I am a bit of a sucker for high quality, custom hunting kit made by craftsmen and artisans who work with natural materials and really know their trade, and some years ago I converted to handmade knives. I therefore have a sheath on my belt with a matching drop-point knife and gut hook made for me by Alan Wood. Not strictly necessary, but gorgeous to handle and use. In the right pocket of my stalking jacket there is also a Victorinox 'Hunter' knife which has both a particularly useful fine, narrow blade and a folding saw.

In my left pocket is my buttolo call on its lanyard, together with a length of thin polypropylene rope which I use for suspending any muntjac I shoot from the nearest suitable tree whilst gralloching. There is also a head torch, which is essential for dealing with any animals shot at last light. Zipped into one side pocket is a supply of latex gloves and a couple of metres of red and white plastic marker tape – very useful for tying to a convenient branch if it becomes necessary to mark the position of a carcass which you, or more particularly a colleague or helper, are going to pick up later. Zipped into a pocket on the other side is my 'jac-strap' muntjac carrier, while in a further zipper pocket I keep a simple first aid kit, a copy of my stalking permission and a photocopy of my firearm certificate. I accept that according to the strict letter of the law, a police officer could, if he or she so wished, demand to see my original FAC and, were I unable to produce it there and then, my rifle and ammunition could be seized. However, most police officers these days are content that a photocopy represents reasonable evidence that you are indeed a certificate holder. Moreover, they will usually agree that the best place for a valuable document is in a secure place at home, not in a muddy field.

Clothing

I have two stalking jackets. Both are in camouflage patterns, Goretex-lined and waterproof, but one is a lightweight coat which I wear in late spring, summer and early autumn when the weather is warm. For the winter months I have a much heavier coat to keep out the cold. At an appropriate moment, as the weather dictates, I transfer all my stalking kit from one to the other, ensuring that it goes into the equivalent pockets so that I know automatically where to reach for any particular item.

Some people do not like camouflage because of concerns that they might be mistaken for an armed terrorist. This is, I agree, a consideration that must be taken into account, especially in locations where there is open public access to woodlands. Personally I think that camouflaged clothing does give the hunter an advantage, and I use not only coat and overtrousers, but also a full headnet and gloves, the latter being particularly important to reduce the visibility of my hands as I raise and lower my binoculars or rifle.

Camouflaged clothing does not turn a bad hunter into a good one, but it will give a competent hunter additional advantage over his quarry

Equally important, clothing-wise, are the inner layers which keep in the warmth, especially on those bitter mornings when you have to wait in a high seat from before dawn in temperatures several degrees below zero. In these circumstances I wear long merino wool underwear, a thick shirt, breeks and woollen stockings, plus a fleece and an additional body warmer under my coat and overtrousers. This usually does the trick, but it is equally important to use well insulated stalking boots, for cold feet are an utter misery.

When the countryside is covered in snow, then white camouflage can offer the stalker significant advantage. After a fresh snowfall deer sometimes appear to be disorientated, and if you are suitably dressed, then it may be possible to stalk much more effectively than is usually the case, provided there is sufficient soft snow to enable movement to be quiet.

When there is significant snow cover, snow camouflage can be very effective indeed

In most winters we do not have many days in southern England with significant snow cover, but when we do, I wear a light snow suit over my winter clothing plus a white woolen ski hat and I have found this to be very effective indeed.

Optics

It is impossible to stalk without good, reliable optics, and quite frankly the more you are able to invest in these, the better. There are a small number of high quality manufacturers, mostly German or Austrian, and their products are significantly better than those of the rest of the field. They are also significantly more expensive, but you only need to buy good optics once: thereafter they will last a lifetime.

When choosing a riflescope for shooting a species like muntjac, which you will usually be spotting at close range in woodland, the emphasis

The ideal binoculars for muntjac stalking should be of relatively low power, but with excellent light gathering capability

must be on a wide field of vision coupled with a large objective lens for excellent light gathering. Magnification of between 6 and 8 is ideal, which in fixed magnification parlance, equates to 6x42 or 8x56 if the exit pupil is to be optimised in low light. Anything more powerful, and there is a good chance, as you mount your rifle, of failing to pick up in your scope the small, moving target which you spotted moments earlier crossing the ride ahead. If you favour using a variable powered scope, set the power ring to around 7. Illuminated reticles are a very valuable aid for the muntjac hunter, and indeed for all stalkers operating at dawn and dusk under the heavy shadow of a woodland canopy. Better still are those scopes with an automatic cut-out which switches off the reticle after the scope has been stationary for a set period of say, two hours, or when it is not positioned in a shooting attitude. I invariably used to forget to turn off my manually operated illuminated reticle and was constantly replacing riflescope batteries or worse, turning on my scope before dawn upon my arrival in the woods to find that my battery was dead. That is no longer the case, thanks to this useful bit of technology on my Zeiss riflescope.

When you start stalking in the near darkness of early morning, turn the illuminated reticle to a low setting so that the sight picture in your scope is not overwhelmed by the intensity of the aiming dot or cross, then gradually increase the brilliance as the light level rises. When there is sufficient daylight for you to position your aiming point on a target without the need for illumination, turn the power off, or if you prefer, switch to a bright daylight setting if your scope has one available.

Likewise you should select binoculars which have a wide field of vision and thus a relatively low power of around x8, which is significantly less than might be appropriate for spotting red deer on the Scottish hill. They should be sufficiently lightweight that they can be held one-handed and used almost constantly whilst you are stalking. Rubber armouring is essential in order both to protect the optics and to eliminate any noise made by the minor knocks and bumps against your stalking sticks or other objects that will surely occur in the field. As with riflescopes, buy the best you can afford from one or other of the top manufacturers, and look upon your binoculars as a long term investment. I currently use a pair of Swarovski EL 8.5x42 binoculars. Their ergonomic design makes them very comfortable to use one-handed, and they combine optical excellence with the ideal degree of magnification.

Carcass Extraction

One of the many joys of shooting muntjac is that, because of their diminutive size, they are such a delight to deal with once on the deck. As any experienced stalker will confirm, it's not taking the shot that is usually the difficult part about shooting deer; it's what comes afterwards that constitutes the hard work. But muntjac, unlike fallow or red deer, take only a few moments to gralloch and can be carried with ease back to the vehicle. Nothing is required by way of specialist machinery, there is no back-breaking drag or the lifting of huge carcasses to worry about, and that is a significant consideration seeing as the average age of the recreational stalker now hovers close to 50 years.

There are, however, a few simple gadgets or accessories which can make moving and handling muntjac carcasses easier, and which can assist in ensuring that carcasses are delivered to the larder cleanly, hygienically and in the best condition.

The most basic of these is the length of thin rope which I carry in the pocket of my stalking jacket, which I use to hoist a deer into a suitable tree for gralloching and field preparation. Once the gralloch is complete, and with one end of the rope secured through the hocks, bind the two hind legs firmly

If the legs are tied together, a muntjac can be carried out of the woods with a convenient pole to act as a handle

together and tie off, before proceeding to secure the two front legs together at the knees. Then, by a process of looping the remainder of the rope back and forth between the secured front and rear legs, you can create a 'handle' by which a muntjac carcass can easily be carried by a singlehanded stalker.

If there are two people available, then another option is to find a suitable pole lying in the woods which can be slipped between the secured front and rear legs so that the animal can be carried between the two stalkers like a sedan chair.

Even easier is my leather muntjac carrier or 'jac-strap'. This can be easily made up by any saddler or leather worker, or home-made if you have access to a suitable piece of leather and a local shoe-repairer to do the stitching. All that is needed is a broad strap which is divided lengthwise at each end for about 20cm and which has four brass 'D' rings fitted to the loose ends. By looping one of the straps around each foot, the carcass can be slung over a shoulder and carried with ease. The 'jac-strap' is light, it rolls up to fit in my pocket and above all, it is simple, which appeals to me.

Loop one loose end of the strap around each foot

The 'jac-strap' keeps both hands free when carrying a muntjac, and rolls up to pocket size when not in use

If the 'jac-strap' and the rope carrier have any disadvantage, then it is that the carcass is not fully contained, and any blood leaking out of it is apt to distribute itself on clothing and equipment. Likewise if the carcass is not handled with some care, then it could potentially become soiled. That is not the case if it is enclosed in a leakproof bag of some sort. One area where I shoot muntjac with a group of colleagues is a nature reserve owned by a conservation charity. It has constant public access and because of this we do not gralloch in the woods. This means that carcasses to be extracted are nearly half as heavy again as the gralloched animals that would normally be so easy to lift and carry. In order to avoid leaving blood trails through the woods, especially in frosty or snowy weather, any carcasses which are dragged are laced into a tough PVC-coated canvas drag bag.

A further option is the use of a roe sack. This puts the entire weight of any carcass across the shoulders, making it very easy to carry. Roe sacks are many and varied in their design, but most will come with a waterproof liner that can be removed and washed out. Most will also have various pockets and pouches in which additional items of kit may be stowed. If I have one reservation about using a roe sack it is that if you are stalking on foot rather than sitting in a high seat, then you have to carry the roe sack on your back while you are actively hunting. If you chance upon a muntjac, there is most unlikely to be time to prepare yourself by removing the roe sack from your shoulders, as the shot will probably have to be taken almost immediately. That means one of the shoulder straps will at best interpose itself between your shooting coat and the butt of your rifle when you raise the rifle to your shoulder, with the consequence that your gun mount will be altered and, in the case of a thick shoulder strap, quite considerably altered. For some stalkers that is not a problem, but personally I feel uncomfortable about anything which can potentially change, even quite subtly, stock length or eye relief.

This roe sack by Monarch Country Products has a washable liner and plenty of spare pockets for stalking kit

Napier's 'Apex Predator' converts into a shoulder sack sufficiently large to carry two muntjac

Hunting kit manufacturers are an innovative lot, however, and one of the latest accessories to be introduced to the market circumvents the problem of having to stalk in what is effectively a shoulder harness. When not in use for carrying game, Napier's 'Apex Predator' is worn around the waist, either in front or behind, like a 'bumbag'. It has four useful zippered pouches for your gralloching kit or other accessories.

A plastic carcass tray prevents blood and dirt from contaminating your vehicle

After a successful shot, however, and with the addition of a pair of carrying straps, the bag quickly converts into a shoulder sack large enough to carry two muntjac. It may feel a little bulky when being worn around the waist, but it does not excessively restrict body movement and the first time I took it into the field, I was certainly very grateful to have it with me after shooting two muntjac in a wood with notoriously bad access and where two inches of rain on heavy clay soil had dismissed any thought of bringing up a vehicle. With the help of a strong drawstring, both animals were secured comfortably in the waterproof liner and carrying their combined weight of 21.5kg a mile back to the land rover was a breeze.

5 A MUNTJAC STALKING PHILOSOPHY

Fifty years ago, roe deer in Britain were regarded as little more than vermin. They were detested by foresters and gunned down with shotguns on organised drives in which as many deer were wounded and lost as were killed. Today, attitudes towards roe have changed. While there is universal acceptance that they must be managed, the manner of such management now shows respect towards the species. The close seasons appropriate to the roe's annual cycle are well understood and the restrictions on the firearms and ammunition which may be used to shoot roe are properly observed. Even though most of the roe we see today in England and Wales owe much of their ancestry to the legacy of introductions from overseas, it is recognised that they have a place in the British countryside.

That place, moreover, has been further guaranteed by the thrill and challenge that is offered by the relatively new sport of woodland roe stalking. As I have already observed, one of the benefits of organised field sports is that they confer status upon quarry species. Responsible and ethical hunters develop huge respect for the creatures which they hunt, and the more difficult or complex it is to kill or take a particular quarry animal or bird, the greater the respect in which it is held, that respect being passed on from hunter to hunter down the generations. Dedicated hunters also devote considerable amounts of time and energy as well as substantial financial resources towards their sport, and thus they see to it that their quarry is not abused. Because of the commitment they make, and as a result of the aggregated respect that has been conferred upon the quarry animal or bird over time by the hunting community, that quarry attains a value which helps to ensure its continued survival. Consider the grey partridge. If it were not for the esteem in which this species is held by the game shooting community and the huge efforts made by shooting estates to conserve it, then the species would quite likely by now have disappeared from the British countryside.

Likewise, when a landowner or an estate derives valuable income from those seeking high quality stalking experiences, then attitudes to deer can change quite quickly. Control at all costs may be replaced by sustainable management and perhaps even a desire to improve the quality of the local population through selective culling. That is what has happened in Britain with roe deer, though it has taken half a century for us to get where we are today. Now perhaps it is for those who value muntjac as a sporting species to drive forward the principles of responsible and ethical management which, while doing the job of control that is rightly demanded by farmers, foresters and landowners, confer more respect upon the species.

A Challenging Quarry

Certainly my own personal respect for these little deer has grown hugely over the years that I have been stalking them seriously, and much of that respect has developed because they are such a challenging quarry to hunt. Rarely do muntjac stand still. Whether you are sitting in a high seat or stalking quietly along a ride, your first glimpse will often be of an animal on the move. Maybe

Rarely do muntjac stand still – your first glimpse will often be of an animal on the move

it will be walking purposefully across open ground between one wood and another or perhaps it will be crossing a ride, hesitating here and there for a moment to take a bite of food. Either way, if you wish to get a shot, you will need to react quickly, decisively, and with quiet efficiency. Occasionally when I put roe stalking friends in a high seat for a chance at muntjac I will find that, although they may have seen an animal that was in range and which presented a safe backstop, they have not taken a shot simply because it did not remain still for long enough. Instead of standing broadside on in the approved manner in order to allow them time to assess the range, sex and age class of the animal with the assistance of binoculars and then take the opportunity to settle into the shot and carefully squeeze the trigger, the pesky muntjac has simply walked on into the undergrowth.

It is the same for overseas guests who come to England to shoot their first muntjac. They tend to be used to larger deer and are usually surprised at how small muntjac are. Suddenly faced with a tiny target that does not stand still and wait to be shot at, visiting hunters often struggle to hit them in the right place.

It is of course possible to stop a muntjac with a sharp whistle or a squeak on the Buttolo call, but the animal will not stop for long, and I find it far preferable to put the riflescope straight onto it, quickly check its status as a potential target and then track it and wait for that fatal moment's hesitation. This requires fluid, confident shooting and of course it also requires a more or less immediate safety assessment. When shooting from a high seat, the matter of safe backstop is generally covered off, but when stalking at ground level it is not, although basic geometry dictates that a small target close to the ground and observed at relatively short range, as muntjac usually are, will often tend to offer a safe shot if taken from a standing position off sticks.

When a muntjac is on the move through the undergrowth of the forest floor, then it may be difficult to get a sufficiently clear view of it to make a shot possible. Perhaps the first you see of an animal is a flicker of movement through a hazel coppice or carpet of low bramble. You can see that the muntjac is walking, possibly quite quickly, but you also realise that it is not possible to get an unobstructed shot. In those circumstances I look ahead of the animal and try to pick a gap in the trees or undergrowth through which it is likely to pass. Then, with my riflescope trained on the gap, I wait for the muntjac to walk into my line of fire.

Females: To Shoot or Not to Shoot?

Quick decision making is assisted by the fact that muntjac have no close season. There is therefore no need to check long and hard through the binoculars in the way that one might in order to look for telltale lumps on the head of a young fallow buck or the anal tush at the rear end of a Christmas roe doe. Any muntjac will be lawful quarry at whatever time of the year you wish to shoot it. The question of whether you decide to pull the trigger on any animal is thus a personal one. To some extent it is conditioned by the circumstances of the stalking opportunity you are presented with. Sometimes – quite often in my experience – the landowner will expect you to shoot any muntjac on sight. Unfortunately because of year-round breeding, this can potentially result in dependent fawns being orphaned. Since young fawns are generally hidden deep in obscuring vegetation, there is usually no opportunity to shoot both the doe and an accompanying fawn, though I have on occasion shot a doe together with a dependant fawn no bigger than a leveret. It is not a particularly enjoyable thing to do.

Above: Female muntjac are always in season, even during the summer

Right: This heavily pregnant doe was a perfect animal to cull

So the stalker is generally left with a dilemma. Do you shoot a doe that shows obvious signs of recently having given birth simply because the forester, farmer or estate owner who has invited you onto the land regards it as just another muntjac which needs shooting? Or do you spare her and avoid the probability of leaving a young fawn to starve or be taken by the local fox population?

From the perspective of the professional stalker or deer manager, while it is a nice idea not to shoot thin does and to shoot only heavily pregnant ones, this is not so easy in practice, especially if there is a big cull figure to be achieved. The reality is that the nuances of a muntjac's pregnancy status are quite hard to identify under field conditions, in poor light and in thick cover, thus when a stalker is under pressure to cull a lot of them, the tendency is to take the shot. Inevitably a few fawns are orphaned, but young muntjac are actually very good survivors. Because their dam, almost from the moment that she gives birth, is putting all her energy into nurturing another fawn, they must be capable of being self-sufficient from a very early age. One professional stalker on an estate which shoots some 200 muntjac a year tells me how he shot a doe and saw a young fawn run away. He did not shoot it, and the fawn survived and grew, thereafter always being seen in the same place.

My personal approach depends largely upon circumstances and upon the landowner's wishes, but on my own regular stalking ground where I am able to determine management strategy in the longer term, my tendency is to spare a doe if I can immediately see that she is obviously thin and has only recently given birth. However much we may be conditioned to shoot what others regard as vermin, I never find it entirely comfortable to gralloch a doe that is heavy in milk and which I know full well has a fawn nearby.

Quick Reactions

Just as it is essential to make both a rapid assessment of safety and selection of quarry, so it is necessary to make an instant decision over point of aim. Here, in most cases, chest is best. While there may be a strong argument for neck shooting in larger species, the overall size of the target area on a muntjac is considerably smaller than that on a roe, and far smaller than that on a fallow or red deer. Couple this observation with the need to shoot quickly and instinctively, perhaps with a standing shot off sticks at an animal which may

Muntjac will rarely wait while you check them out with the binoculars, and they are a small and challenging target

be stationary for only a few moments, and it becomes clear that the chest shot offers an acceptable margin for error in circumstances where the neck shot does not. There is one situation, though, in which I regularly take a neck shot, and that is when a muntjac is walking directly away from me. In this case, with the rifle on a solid rest such as the shooting rail of a high seat or, on one memorable occasion, a fallen branch which fortuitously happened to be on the ground in front of me as I lay prone, I watch the backside of the animal through my riflescope and wait for it to stick out its head at ninety degrees in order to snatch a bite of food, as it will invariably do while it walks away. Then I shoot down its flank into the base of the neck.

The challenge of having to make quick and positive decisions is one of the things I find so enthralling about shooting muntjac. Nevertheless, it is important always to shoot within the limits of one's capabilities and, equally importantly, to know what those capabilities are and how they will change according to the light level or the position from which a shot is to be taken. A stalker may be comfortable taking a shot early in the evening from a high seat that he would not attempt off the sticks at last light. With experience comes confidence, and with confidence comes the willingness to attempt more difficult shots. That to my mind is perfectly acceptable, for it is all part of developing personal proficiency – provided that you still recognise the limits of your abilities and remain within them.

On occasions I take a shot at a moving target, when a muntjac is comfortably within range, clearly visible and walking purposefully without showing any signs of hesitation. Moving targets do not fall within the regular canon of shooting experience for most UK stalkers in the way that they do for continental hunters, who are comfortable at shooting fast running deer or boar in driven hunts. If I shoot at a moving muntjac it is invariably off a rest and not freehand, which of course is the accepted method when shooting driven game with a rifle. Furthermore I never do so if I do not have a dog available. I can think of only one occasion when a moving shot has gone wrong, and that was late one summer's evening when I was sitting in a high seat in an old orchard. A doe walked out in front of me at about 50 metres and simply kept going. It was clear that she would not be stopping and as the landowner wanted all muntjac shot, I moved the .243 with her and fired. Instantly I knew the shot had gone too far back, and she ran into a dense bed of nettles where I could hear her moving about, obviously still very much alive. As I was close to the edge of the property, it was quickly getting dark and I did not want to risk pushing a wounded deer across the boundary, I left her and returned at first light the following morning with my dog, who found the doe quite dead about twenty metres from where I had last heard her.

The confidence to take a shot quickly is definitely something which regular shooting at muntjac engenders, and it pays off in a variety of other circumstances. One morning I was stalking springbok in South Africa. The professional hunter and I were creeping at dawn down a deep erosion gully, which was the only cover available that would get us anywhere in range of a group of very wary springbok about 350 metres ahead. Carefully we inched our way along the gully, the PH occasionally looking cautiously over the lip of the gully and out across the veldt to see if the animals were still there. At each bend in the gully he peered round with immense caution until, upon checking around a particularly sharp corner, he quickly drew back and whispered urgently: 'Ram on the top, opposite side, 50 metres.'

I pushed the muzzle of the .300 H&H magnum around the earth bank, clocked the ram and fired instantly. As we walked up to the springbok, which

This springbok owed at least part of its downfall to reactions honed by muntjac shooting

lay quite dead on the dry earth, the PH expressed amazement at the speed at which the shot had been taken. I explained how shooting regularly at these small agile beasts we call muntjac is a wonderful way of honing the reactions and reflexes in a hunter.

A Muntjac Stalker's Year

My muntjac stalking year starts in late August when most of the harvest is completed. Muntjac are small animals and when the corn and oilseed rape stands high it can be virtually impossible to see them moving along the headlands and field margins, let alone in the woods, which are dense with vegetation. Once the combines have done their work, however, and the countryside of early autumn is laid bare, visibility returns once more. The same is true in the woodland rides, where the tall grass turns from green to pale yellow, the nettles start to thin and it becomes possible once more to observe wildlife on the move. Perhaps the rides will be mown in readiness for the game shooting season, and if that is the case whole vistas suddenly open up along the woodland floor. An estate where I regularly shoot mows its rides in late summer and this is hugely beneficial from the muntjac stalking perspective. One year no mowing of rides was possible because of the wet ground conditions. As a result the tall undergrowth which stood well into the autumn made stalking much more difficult and had a significant effect upon the year's overall tally. Not only was it far more difficult to spot muntjac, but moving silently along the rides became much more difficult and all too often the first contact with a muntjac was the bark of a departing animal as it ran off into the wood. While ground cover remains dense, the high seat remains the most practical way of shooting.

Early autumn is a particularly beautiful time in the woods, and as the days draw in towards the equinox, a morning stalk no longer demands getting up at such an excruciating hour as is faced by the midsummer roebuck stalker. Very often I will spend the first hour in a high seat and then go for a walk through the woods as the sun comes up. Although all other deer will most likely have by then retreated into dense cover, there will quite often be muntjac on the move at this time, and it is not unusual to encounter them walking through the woods even a couple of hours after sunrise. Scientific observation has suggested that muntjac are active for a longer period at dusk than they are at dawn, which is a very good argument for stalking in the evening. Nevertheless, the bulk of my outings are in the morning, largely because the countryside is quieter at that time and there is less disturbance.

It is difficult to spot muntjac in summer before the crops are harvested

Early autumn is a
beautiful time to
be in the woods

At dawn, especially in early autumn, few other people are up and about. Even the stockmen, gamekeepers and vermin catchers will not have begun their rounds until after sunrise and there is little traffic on the country roads. The air is cool and still, and it is a sheer delight to be hunting at such a time of day. Besides, a morning outing fits well with my other responsibilities and if I am stalking locally, then I can be finished and washed up in the larder by mid morning and able to turn my attention to other matters. Thus the day has been extended. An evening outing, on a weekday at least, means curtailing the working day and heading to the woods before foresters, gamekeepers and others have finished their work. There are more likely to be members of the public using footpaths and bridleways, and the countryside is just that much busier. Even so, if an evening outing fits in with my schedule, then I will not turn down the opportunity.

Until leaf fall is well underway, the woodland floor is still largely obscured and spotting deer is not at all easy. Furthermore, while the ground is still hard, there is less opportunity to study tracks, trails and slot marks. I thus make occasional outings during this period, but ensure that all available woods are visited, which at least enables me to check out any changes which have occurred over the summer.

Late autumn and winter provide prime opportunity for getting muntjac into the larder. I usually try to make a concerted effort towards the end of October, setting out high seats in a number of favoured spots and then visiting them morning and evening over a period of a few days. Late autumn and winter, however, is also the most important period in the game shooting calendar, and any stalking activity can only take place if it has the support of the shoot manager and gamekeeper.

Attitudes can vary greatly. Some keepers are quite happy for the stalker to be out and about in the woods during the shooting season, because they understand full well that a competent and responsible stalker will not disturb game. If the stalker disturbs gamebirds, then he will most certainly be disturbing deer too, thus making his visit rather pointless. Other keepers, though, do not want anyone but themselves anywhere near their birds at least until after Christmas, and that can make any attempt to fulfill the landowner's desire to control muntjac very frustrating. These matters are best solved by direct discussion. Get the shoot dates diarised so that they can be avoided. If there is a regular weekly shoot day, then arrange for your stalking visits to fall midway between shoots, so that the woods have had a chance to settle down after the beaters have been through them, but at a time when there can be no question of your having disturbed the coverts immediately prior to a shoot. Where there is a gamekeeper, then I always phone or text him before stalking, and I always take every opportunity to shoot foxes. This works wonders for relations between stalker and gamekeeper.

Winter is also a busy time for forestry operations. If there is a major programme of thinning or felling taking place, then it is bound to cause significant disturbance that will move deer within the woods and even cause them to depart completely. One winter in which significant felling activity occurred on a forestry estate where I stalk saw the muntjac vanish almost entirely. When I discussed this with the gamekeeper, he agreed that they had moved out of the main coverts and were instead lying up in the outlying hedges and spinneys where he had encountered them on his feeding rounds. Of course major forestry work is usually planned in advance and projected operations may be checked with the landowner or forester. It may be necessary to move high seats to enable the passage of machinery or the felling of timber.

During the short days of winter, it is worth maximising the amount of time spent in the woods

Briefing the rifles prior to a group cull. These events require a great deal of hard work and organisation, but they can prove very successful

During the dark days of mid-winter, days are so short that it becomes profitable to make a morning outing, go for lunch in the pub and then straight out again into the woods. Five or six hours can be devoted to stalking and there is little wasted down-time. Thus in December I try to make at least a couple of full day visits to a more distant stalking ground where it makes sense to maximise the time spent stalking in relation to that spent travelling.

My busiest period of muntjac stalking is usually the few weeks that follow the close of the game shooting season. The woods are now relatively undisturbed, except for Saturday evenings in February, when beaters are traditionally permitted to shoot roosting woodpigeons. At the same time, the ground cover is at its lowest and there is excellent visibility. This is the season, in late February or early March, in which I usually try to organise a group cull, inviting a few stalking friends to hunt morning and evening over a period of three days or so. It is quite a lot of hard work, setting out six or eight extra high seats and then arranging for them to be filled for those crucial dawn and dusk hours, perhaps by a succession of rifles. It usually fills the larder, however, and a detailed report to the landowner at the end of the operation demonstrates commitment to killing muntjac on his property.

The results of a group cull hang in the larder

If there is a wood in which I know there to be muntjac present, but where the group cull has failed to make an impression, I will leave any temporary portable high seats out for an extra couple of weeks and then come back for a few additional sessions myself. It is quite surprising how often this approach can bag an extra two or three animals.

In April the dog's mercury will be clothing the woodland floor in a fresh green carpet while there usually starts to appear a dusting of green along the hedgerows and in the hazel copse. Birdsong in the woods is at its most glorious in the magical hour around dawn, and then in May come the bluebells and bud-burst. Quickly, visibility through the layer of ground cover closest to the woodland floor becomes obscured and by the end of the month it starts to become more difficult to spot muntjac easily when stalking on foot. In these circumstances shooting from high seats positioned close to clearings and open rides may be more productive.

On a bed of evergreen. In Britain we do not usually offer a shot animal the 'last bite' as continental hunters do, but this fine buck deserves respect – and the fir fronds help to make a nice photograph

Conversely, it is during the summer, when flower beds are blooming and vegetable plots are in full production, that gardeners experience most muntjac damage and thus it is not unusual at this time to receive requests from those with large gardens and shrubberies to remove an offending animal.

Such requests highlight the differences in attitudes towards the species which provides so many muntjac hunters with the opportunity to participate in this branch of deer stalking. To the gardener with a bed full of trashed busy lizzies or a row of chomped courgettes, the guilty muntjac is a personal enemy. To the muntjac hunter like myself, however, these creatures are a fascinating sporting challenge. Moreover, they are capable of bringing the reality of lowland deer stalking right to the doorsteps of an increasing number of sporting shooters.

6 VIEW FROM A HIGH SEAT

Many aspects of the relatively new sport of woodland stalking have been imported from continental Europe, and the use of high seats is one of them. The traditional pattern for the high seat in central Europe is the enclosed tower, most being situated on the edges of woods in positions where they will command a view of any roe, red deer or wild boar that emerges from cover into the neighbouring fields. These towers provide total concealment for the waiting hunter plus protection against the elements, something which is particularly useful in a cold climate.

More often, the high seats we use in the UK are exposed lean-to structures, positioned against convenient trees overlooking rides or clearings that are favoured by deer. I know some stalkers who dislike sitting in high seats. They find it boring to sit still in the same place for two hours or more, and would much prefer to be on the move, stalking on foot. Both strategies can be successful of course, but there is no doubt that when it comes to putting muntjac in the bag, the use of high seats can be very beneficial, and if I look back over my own stalking records I can see that the number of muntjac I shoot from high seats regularly outweighs the number shot from ground level, even if it is the successful stalks on foot which are often the more memorable hunting experiences.

Position high seats where they can be used to monitor regular muntjac paths

Where muntjac population density is low, waiting in a high seat is usually the best means of focussing effort on the most likely places. Likewise if there is a requirement to shoot a particular animal, perhaps because it is raiding a vegetable garden or maybe because it carries a medal trophy head, then a high seat may be used to take advantage of the fact that muntjac are creatures of habit and that they operate within defined territories.

At certain times of the year, high seats provide a more practical means of getting on terms with muntjac. Once ground cover has thickened up in the spring, a good way to get an unobstructed view of such a small animal is from the elevated vantage point of a high seat, and between bud burst and mid autumn, high seat shooting has a distinct advantage. During the winter, when group culls are being organised, the use of high seats is the only practical way of accommodating a number of stalkers in the same wood or on the same estate at any one time, and provided that stalkers are detailed to operate from them, there is no need for the cull organiser to supply a comprehensive geographical brief to each individual participant. A guest stalker, even if he

When the ground cover has thickened up, a high seat can provide the best means of getting an unobstructed view of a small deer like a muntjac

does not know the ground, can be confident that from a well-sited high seat there will be as reasonable an opportunity as any of seeing deer, and that a shot taken in the shooting zone around the seat will be a safe one. Likewise the host can be assured that an experienced stalker, once guided to the seat, has a good chance of contributing to the cull and will not get lost, stray into forbidden ground or wander across property boundaries.

Perfect Positioning

Siting high seats for muntjac shooting requires a bit of thought, for the ground they need to command will be different from that which the roe shooter might wish to observe. While roe will move with confidence out of the woods at dusk into open fields to feed, muntjac tend to stay tighter to the woodland edge, remaining close to the dense cover of bramble beds, thickets, scrub or hedgerows, so rather than placing a seat on the edge of a wood where it looks out over wide vistas, it can be better to concentrate on suitable positions within the wood itself, such as rides, small clearings or even simply places where the trees are less dense and it is possible to get a good view of the woodland floor. When I think of my best high seat positions for muntjac, they are all within the wood rather than on the edge of it.

Like other wild creatures, muntjac use regular paths through woodland, and it makes a good deal of sense to position high seats where one or more favourite routes can be monitored from them. On one estate where I shoot regularly, the rides are usually bounded by ditches across which there are very clear muntjac crossing points. I try to have at least a couple of these crossing places within sight of a high seat, but it is equally important for regular deer paths to be within comfortable shooting range. There is no point in being able to watch the same muntjac crossing a ride each morning if it is no more than a small dot in the riflescope.

Study the habitat within your stalking area and, in selecting possible sites for high seats, focus on the dense areas which are favoured by muntjac or on those places through which muntjac travel when moving back and forth between their favourite spots. A particularly successful seat from which I have shot many muntjac overlooks a dense area of hazel coppice. Not only is the habitat particularly favourable, but the open areas between the coppice stools afford plenty of visibility, and it is not difficult to spot muntjac patrolling the

area and then get a clear shot at them as they pass between the stools. In another wood where I shoot, there is a point at which a long strip of fairly open-floored mature mixed woodland sits between two dense blocks of young broadleaf thicket. Muntjac cross between these two thickets, passing through the more mature wood as they do so, and it is here where I position my high seat, about 70 metres back from the favourite crossing point. There is only one place in this wood which offers optimum visibility and the place in question has no convenient tree to lean a seat against, so when shooting this beat I use a free-standing portable high seat complete with a set of legs.

Portable seats are extremely useful, both when determining where to position a more permanent seat and when mounting short campaigns or culls. I have used folding portables for years, and there are now telescopic extending portables on the market which can easily be back-packed into position. If there is a set of legs available, however, a portable becomes even more useful, as it can then be placed precisely in the best spot to ensure good lines of sight for shooting, irrespective of whether or not there is a perfectly-placed tree to lean it against.

Above: Try to ensure that a couple of well-used tracks or crossing points are visible from and within range of a high seat position

Right: Portable seats are extremely useful, especially when used with a leg kit. This position enables the shooter to see clearly down three rides

While a high seat can place the hunter in a good place to see deer, keeping him above both the eye level and scenting level of his quarry whilst also offering confidence that any shot that is taken has a safe backstop, a high seat does not necessarily provide concealment – unless it is like one of those fully enclosed continental shooting cabins on stilts. If you want to stay unobserved, then it is important to remain still.

One evening I was sitting in my folding portable seat, which I had positioned earlier that day against a favourite oak tree from which there is a clear view down rides both in front of me and to my right. It was late winter, I had been seated for an hour and a half and it was starting to get dark and cold. Even though I knew that there were plenty of muntjac using the area, plus the occasional fallow, the evening had been entirely blank and my vigil had started to become tedious. My right leg was getting a little stiff, so I moved my foot from the top rung of the high seat where it was resting in order to stretch my ankle. As I did so, I heard the rustle of dead leaves just 20 metres behind

Top Left: A telescopic portable high seat can easily be back-packed into position

Top Right: The telescopic portable in use

me as a muntjac scampered away and, turning to take a look, I was treated to the sight of a white tail bouncing away into the gloom of the wood.

On another occasion I was hoping for a muntjac to get my season's cull underway after harvest had been gathered in. Since long before dawn I had been sitting in one of my favourite places, a high, galvanised seat in a position from which I have shot many deer over a period of fourteen years, but again I had seen precisely nothing. The seat itself is some 4 metres above ground level and in early autumn I had leafy branches all around, but that did not prevent a muntjac from spotting me as I turned my head a little too quickly to check out the ground to my right. Again, there was the rustle of leaves, again the white flag, again the annoyance and frustration at a wasted opportunity, for in both cases, had I been more careful, a shot could potentially have presented itself.

There are other times, however, when I have had muntjac walk so close to my high seat that I could have almost reached out and touched them.

Above: Grass and bracken has been mown in early autumn, making it much easier to spot any muntjac which walks out onto the ride in front of this well-camouflaged seat

Right: Feed rides and pheasant feeders around release pens can be good places to ambush muntjac

Close Encounters

It was towards the end of March that I was sitting in a high seat very early in the morning on the edge of a woodland ride which is criss-crossed by deer paths and which regularly produces shooting opportunities for me. As the first grey streaks of daylight filtered through the bare branches to ground level, a muntjac doe walked out of the wood from behind me no more than 15 metres away. Watching her out of the corner of my eye, I could see that, instead of stepping into the open and crossing the ride, she was walking slowly along the edge of the tree line, directly towards where I was sitting. To have turned towards her with the rifle would have alerted her, so I sat perfectly still and waited.

Steadily she crept towards me, hesitating for a moment just feet away, then moving onwards until she was directly under my high seat, exactly beneath where I was sitting. She had actually stepped between the legs of the seat and the tree against which it was leaning. Knowing that she could not possibly see me, I used this brief moment to move my rifle and, guessing that she would emerge from below me, proceed on her course and walk away, I positioned it so as to take a shot when she had got out to about 20 metres. Having successfully executed this manoeuvre in total silence, I was confident of putting her in the bag until, a moment later, there came a scrabbling of leaves and twigs from below me. The starting of an alarmed muntjac was quickly followed by a retreating shape which retraced its steps and darted back into the wood in exactly the place from whence it had come.

She had not seen me, she had not heard me, and my scent was well above her head, so why had she run? I thought about it for a moment and then realised that she must have got the hand scent from my stalking sticks which I had left leaning against the tree when I had ascended the high seat. Some stalkers recommend that you should bring your sticks aloft into a high seat with you. I have never done so, but most certainly that would have prevented this particular doe from being alerted to my presence. The blank was saved twenty minutes later, however, when a fallow pricket walked out into the ride at the much more comfortable range of 60 metres.

Another series of close encounters occurred a month afterwards. I had left a free-standing portable seat out at the intersection of two rides in a wood where I had organised a cull the previous month. Nobody had enjoyed any success from that particular seat during the cull despite the fact that there were plenty of signs of muntjac in the wood, so it seemed a good plan to leave the seat in position, wait until the dust had settled and then spend another morning there.

I'm glad I did so. Approaching the high seat in the very earliest glimmer of dawn, I caught a movement in my binoculars. It was still very dark at ground level and it took a while to identify the shadowy shape, but close observation confirmed that it was a muntjac doe, walking towards me. I set up the rifle on the sticks, eventually picked her up in the scope and waited for her to present a suitable target. Luckily at 25 metres she did so, turning broadside past a clump of daffodils against which she was neatly silhouetted. I heard the thump of the .243 bullet striking her, waited for a moment and then walked forward to check the ground. There was nothing to be seen beside the daffodil clump, but I knew she could not be far away and, not wishing to cause any further disturbance, I retreated to the high seat which was now 30 metres to my right, climbed the ladder and waited.

About half an hour later I spotted a muntjac buck. I had not seen him come out of cover, but there he was, standing on the ride just 15 metres away, looking straight at me, eyeball to eyeball. For what seemed like an eternity but was in reality about five minutes I didn't so much as move a muscle, indeed I hardly dared breathe in case a plume of vapour emerging through my camo headnet into the chill morning air might betray the fact that I was a living being and not merely a lump of leaf-coloured debris perched up a ladder in the middle of a wood. The buck repeatedly tested the air with his nose, advanced a pace, hesitated, tested again and then retreated. This game went on until, quite suddenly, the buck seemed to have decided that I represented no threat after all, whereupon he ambled towards me, turned through ninety degrees at the foot of the high seat and proceeded to walk directly away.

Now at last, with the buck's gaze focussed ahead of him, I had the chance to raise, ever so slowly, the rifle on the shooting rail in front of me and to lower my head until I could see the back and hindquarters of the retreating muntjac, waiting for the moment when he would turn his neck and head to one side or the other. In the split second that he did so, I positioned the red dot at the base of his neck and squeezed the trigger. He dropped where he stood.

A further fifteen minutes passed, whereupon another doe stepped out of the wood beside me. This time she was facing away from me, with her head up, looking across the ride, and I was able quietly to move the rifle round and look straight down at the back of her head, just 20 metres away, place the reticle on the top of her neck and take a simple shot.

My old Labrador bitch, Pintail, found the first doe very quickly for me. It had run into the wood, leaving only a few specks of blood for me to follow but plenty of lovely scent for a dog's nose to savour, and by the time I got up to where she had stopped, about 40 metres back into cover, she was gleefully licking at and dancing around the dead animal. What she really appreciated, however, were the tasty titbits of no fewer than three muntjac hearts shot from animals at a total combined range of about 65 metres.

All three muntjac that morning were an object lesson in close range shooting: wear a head net and gloves, trust to your camouflage and don't move a hair while the animal is looking in your direction. A high seat may put you out of scent of a deer, but it does not make you invisible, and the slightest unguarded movement will give you away. Move your rifle only when the deer is either facing away or when its line of sight is interrupted, perhaps as it passes behind a tree. Remember these simple rules and successful close-up shooting is both easy and hugely satisfying. Indeed, I find that there is just as much pure hunting challenge in cleanly killing a deer that is only feet away from me and entirely oblivious to my presence as in decking a hill stag so far away that it is no more than a speck in the 3-12x50.

That morning's shooting was also a demonstration of the fact that a single shot taken from a fixed position does not necessarily clear every muntjac from the vicinity, and that it is quite possible to shoot two, three or even more animals at a sitting, provided that you remain quiet and that you do not move from your position or cause any disturbance to the ground around you. This was the case even in the old days of unmoderated rifles. I well remember sitting in a high seat in a wood next to a rape field. The crop was under constant attack from woodpigeons and there were a couple of gas bangers going off every few minutes. The muntjac were entirely unfazed by this however, and only seconds after I had shot the first animal in a clearing in front of me, a second walked out into the line of fire of my very noisy .308 and, like its friend, paid the penalty for doing so. Presumably it had become accustomed to loud explosions and, to its ultimate cost, had learned to ignore them.

A light scrim surrounding this high seat provides useful cover for its occupant

Garden Raiders

Occasionally I receive calls from local people, usually the owners of small farms or large gardens, who are fed up with a muntjac that is raiding their vegetable crops or herbaceous borders. It is always interesting to make a site visit, to deduce where the offending animal is coming from and to identify the best place from which to get a clear, safe shot at it and when a carefully considered and well-executed tactical plan to ambush a marauding muntjac goes like clockwork, it is hugely satisfying. Invariably a portable high seat comes into play, for within the confines of a small property this offers the only real solution to the ever-present need for a safe backstop.

One August morning I received a call from a lady with a large Georgian house and garden in a nearby market town who was fed up with the muntjac which were raiding her ornamental beds with apparent impunity. I took a walk around the garden with her and quickly concluded that the obvious place to set up my portable seat was against a large cedar tree which overlooked the orchard. The only drawback was that the property was surrounded on three sides by a housing estate, and although the houses were entirely screened from the orchard by a thick belt of trees, from which the muntjac were emerging to invade the garden, the nearest house was no more than 80 metres from the cedar tree against which my seat was positioned.

Bearing in mind the circumstances, I took the precaution of advising the police prior to going shooting. A quick 101 call to the control room ensured that the police had my vehicle registration and mobile telephone number logged against the anticipated time and location of my visit, just in case a worried local resident were to report hearing the sound of a rifle shot. Everything proceeded well. At about eight o'clock on a warm, summer's evening I climbed quietly into position and at eight thirty, just as the occupants of the housing estate were powering up their barbecues for the evening, a muntjac doe duly walked out into the orchard, where a single shot from my moderated .243 put her down on the grass. There was a moment's silence, after which I could hear every door and window in the nearest houses opening, followed by the sound of muted conversation. There was, however, no police siren, and I quietly loaded the carcass into my Land Rover and brought it back to the larder. The property owner was delighted, and I have made several more successful visits there. On each occasion, however, I have been careful to warn the police beforehand.

The Last Patrol

Muntjac are creatures of habit. Territorial bucks in particular can regularly be seen to patrol the same route at the same time of the morning or evening on successive days, and a well placed portable high seat can provide the means of mounting a successful ambush. But of course it has to be positioned in the right place.

I had set up my portable high seat at the top of a favourite little valley which drops from a range of chalk and boulder clay hills down into rolling farmland. There are woods on both sides of the valley, and having spent maybe three quarters of an hour quietly walking the hedgerows elsewhere on the farm, I climbed into the seat at sunset one quiet evening in the hope that something might walk out of cover as darkness fell.

Territorial bucks will patrol the same route at the same time of the morning or evening

For forty minutes or so nothing happened, and I sat looking into the western sky as it turned gradually from orange to pink and then to mauve. Then, when all colour had drained from the landscape and the trees were nothing but grey silhouettes against the dusk, a deer emerged from the wood on my left and stepped down into the valley, taking a steady and determined line for the wood on the hilltop opposite.

It was a muntjac, obviously quite a big, mature buck, but I didn't need a range finder to determine that he was too far away for me even to contemplate a shot. So I watched him as he plodded gently up the opposite hill and disappeared from view in the woodland edge. Within a quarter of an hour it was too dark to shoot and nothing more had shown itself, so I made my way home. That evening I took a look at the map and estimated that the muntjac had crossed the valley some 280 metres from where I had been sitting.

Two days later I found myself in the same place once more. The high seat was still in the same position, and though I had it at the back of my mind that perhaps it might be prudent to move the seat further down the valley, the sun was already slipping below the horizon when I arrived, so I left it where it was and climbed aboard.

Moments later my attention was caught by a fox which trotted out from a group of Scots pines, nosing his way amongst the rabbit holes in search of an evening meal. He had no idea that I was watching him and even less idea that a .308 bullet was heading in his direction, for it struck before the sound of the rifle ever reached his ears. I checked Charlie out with my binoculars and left him where he was, but moments later, satisfaction turned to sheer annoyance and frustration. There, walking slowly once more between the two woods, on that same track 280 metres away, was Mr Muntjac. I had not moved the high seat as had I promised myself that I would, and now the chance of a buck in the bag was slipping once more from my grasp.

In desperation, I climbed down from the seat in full view of the muntjac, crept into the wood on my left and, under cover of the trees, ran as quietly as I could some 150 metres down the flank of the valley before checking cautiously out into the field to my right. The buck was still there, but even though he may not actually have seen me, he must have known that something was not quite right, for he had stopped in his tracks and was already turning to trot back into cover. My chance of a shot was gone.

The western sky turned gradually from orange to pink and then to mauve

I mentally kicked myself for my foolishness and stupidity. Having initially decided to move the high seat to a point which would cover a known muntjac path, I had allowed myself to be distracted from doing so by the antics of a fox. Shooting foxes is all very well, I thought, but while a dead Charlie might win me some points with the keeper, I was there to cull deer, not foxes. It was time to regroup and I decided that having now made my way most of the distance down the valley, I might as well take a walk to the end of the wood in the forlorn hope that perhaps a second muntjac might be on the prowl that evening.

In the high seat, wind direction had been relatively unimportant to me, but now, stalking through the woods at last light, I realised that my scent was being taken by the light breeze across the valley, straight to the place where the muntjac buck had disappeared. Was that a problem? Surely he would not be so foolish as to try and cross once more between the two woods?

I weighed up the prospects in my mind. Certainly the buck had seemed pretty determined, and although my sprint through the trees had obviously spooked him, his cautious reaction suggested that he hadn't actually seen me. More likely he had been alerted by the clatter of a disturbed pigeon. Furthermore, there was only a quarter of an hour of light still available, thus there was little point in starting to stalk new country. So on reflection I retreated to the woodland edge overlooking the valley, sat down on the ground with my back to a sycamore and waited for darkness.

There were no more than three or four minutes of shootable light left when the buck emerged once more, exactly on the same path as he had taken earlier. No doubt about it, this old boy was prepared to let nothing upset his routine and once again he walked at a steady pace down into the valley where a bowl of winter wheat separated the two woods. But this time I was waiting. I let him quarter towards me until he was just 80 metres away and then, in the last grey light of evening and with my rifle tucked comfortably against my left knee, I settled the reticle on his shoulder. A slight intake of breath, the release, the reassuring thump of a bullet striking home and, moments later, I confirmed that the buck was dead on the field in front of me.

His antlers, though unremarkable in terms of measurable quality, were nevertheless a good representative head for a mature animal. They were attractively curved at the tips, though one of the points had been lost, probably in some past fight. Both tusks were broken and battle-worn, the complete closure of the roots suggesting an age of five years at the very least; more likely seven or even more. And he weighed heavily as I carried him back to the land rover in darkness. This old buck had made his last patrol.

7 BOTH FEET ON THE GROUND

For sheer sporting challenge, stalking muntjac on foot takes a lot of beating. The small size of a muntjac and the fact that it will, like as not, be hanging around in dense cover instead of standing out in the open, makes it from the outset a difficult animal to spot. You may perhaps locate roe by finding a vantage point and scanning a roe-friendly landscape with your binoculars, but you are unlikely to locate a muntjac by doing so. The wraith like shapes of a group of fallow may be picked out as they move between the grey boles of a winter woodland, but muntjac are so much smaller that they are, more often than not, obscured by the brambles and brushwood that clothes the forest floor. Just seeing one before it sees you is cause for satisfaction.

Walking the woodland edge, scanning constantly with the binoculars

And if you do manage to observe one, the likelihood is that it will be on the move as muntjac so often are. Unless it is possible to take a shot from where you are standing, there is usually only a slim chance of using the topography and wind direction to stalk to within shooting distance before it has slipped away into some dense thicket and disappeared for good. Most of the time you will be walking slowly along the woodland rides, constantly scanning with the binoculars in the hope that you might creep around a corner and see a deer in front of you or perhaps pick up the movement of an animal as it makes its way across the woodland floor. Maybe a muntjac will be spotted in silhouette patrolling the sunlit edge of the wood as you look out from the dark interior, or slowly discerned on the edge of a ride in the first moments of shootable half-light.

How easy it is to walk right past a muntjac that is couched down in some impenetrable bush or hedgerow. Usually the only indication that you have done this is a sharp rustling of vegetation as the animal springs away unseen. Sometimes there is the brief sight of a white flag, and sometimes a bark of alarm, repeated again and again as the muntjac retreats deep into the wood. If this happens then you know full well that every other deer within earshot has been alerted to the presence of a predator.

Canine Assistance

There is, however, a way of locating a live muntjac if it is deep within cover, even in darkness. My old bitch, Pintail, was a late developer. For the first five years of her life I almost despaired of her becoming the accomplished gundog that her predecessors had been and in whose pawprints I had so dearly hoped she would follow when I bought her as a small puppy. Then, at the age of six, she discovered muntjac. On numerous occasions she made wonderful finds of deer that had run into heavy cover. She located dead muntjac deep within almost impenetrable drifts of bramble and blackthorn and saved me days of painstaking work trying to eyeball blood trails along woodland floors. She also had the ability to wind a nearby muntjac and alert me to where it was. So rather than always leaving her in the back of the land rover as back-up if help was needed to locate a missing deer, I started to have her with me as I stalked.

One morning in late October Pintail and I crept into a familiar wood and started working our way down a narrow ride towards an intersection where I regularly place a high seat. Outside the wood it was barely getting light; inside it was almost pitch dark. The leafy branches meeting over the top of the ride formed what was effectively a dark tunnel that kept the ground vegetation in Stygian gloom. Pintail was on my left, her head just a foot or so in front of me, and we had gone no more than 60 metres into the wood when suddenly she froze, ears pricked in a state of high alert. Thrusting her nose towards the undergrowth to my left, she drew in lungfuls of what was quite clearly the most delicious and exciting scent going. Clearly it was not pheasant, for I knew full well how she behaved when winding gamebirds. It had to be deer.

Equally, I knew that there was not a hope of spotting a muntjac behind a large blackthorn bush in almost pitch darkness. Nevertheless, I too stopped and, in a moment, set up my sticks, placing my rifle on top of them in readiness for whatever might unfold. After maybe twenty seconds came the cracking of twigs and swish of dead leaves from within the blackthorn as the muntjac departed. I could not see it, but I could hear the patter of its feet on the

Pintail's last find before her retirement. This buck took a .308 bullet through the heart but still managed to run over 70 metres into heavy cover before going down. The old girl found him in a matter of seconds

carpet of dead leaves as it circled round behind me and stopped momentarily on the ride, presumably to see what manner of creature had disturbed its slumbers. As it did so, it was perfectly silhouetted by the circle of pale grey dawn light at the end of the tunnel of darkness in which I stood. The doe was facing three-quarters towards me at 60 metres and, picking a point of aim at the front of her right shoulder, I fired without hesitation.

She ran, but she did not run far. Pintail followed her up and found her lying in a heap at the bottom of the big ditch that runs around the outside of the wood. She richly deserved her helping of fresh muntjac heart that morning.

Above: Somebody is waiting for a tasty treat

Right: A proud young Labrador at the start of her stalking career. The first of these bucks dropped where it stood, but Teal made a good find with the second

Those That Wait

In most cases, if a muntjac is seen on the move then it will keep moving. Rarely, I find, do they hang around a particular area and wait to be stalked, unless it is a doe that has a dependent fawn. There are exceptions, however. I recall taking a television crew stalking one morning. They were making a programme about harvesting wild meat from the countryside and then preparing it for the table, a philosophy with which I am in total harmony and which I and my family live by. We had arrived before dawn, and the first grey glimmers of light were showing in the eastern sky as I glassed along the outside edge of a wood and saw a doe retreat into the darkness of the trees just beyond the point where a track emerges from the wood into the adjoining field.

Ushering together the presenter and the cameraman, both of whom were draped with outsize camo gear that I had lent them in order to cover up their bright cagoules, I led them in Indian file down the edge of the wood, then left along the track into the darkness of the woodland canopy, in the hope that we might be able to pick up the muntjac. Amazingly we did just that, for it was still no more than 20 metres inside the wood from where I had first seen it. Except that the doe was not going to hang around and wait for

The first glimmers of light were showing in the eastern sky...

a stalker, a bemused TV presenter and a cameraman. She stood incredulous for a couple of seconds and then did the obvious thing: she barked and white flagged it into the darkness. That brief pause was not time enough for me to let off a shot, but it did, however, give sufficient opportunity for the cameraman to get some lovely footage of an indignant muntjac. I ended up supplying the crew with a selection of pre-packed frozen muntjac fillets and haunches for the kitchen sequence that was to follow. So all turned out well in the end and the programme was a success, even though a muntjac was not actually shot on camera – which in some ways was probably for the best.

There is only one occasion on which I have watched a muntjac couch down and then returned later to stalk it. Whitsun bank holiday weekend had been wet as usual, but by the Monday afternoon the rain had cleared and bright shafts of sunshine were piercing the ragged edges of the clouds. The barley in Five Bricks, the highest field on our farm, was steaming with water vapour as I walked the grass margins around the outside of the field. Installed under a Countryside Stewardship scheme, the margins are left unmown until mid July, and at the end of May the grass was already tall, lush and wet with the recent rain, soaking the dogs' coats as they trotted eagerly alongside me. Rounding a headland at the furthest point of the farm, I saw a muntjac slip out of the barley and into the grass margin. I caught only a glimpse of it, for the crop was sufficiently high to cover the animal completely and its back barely showed above the grass, but it stopped in the margin some hundred metres ahead of me, and very slowly I backed off, hissing the dogs back with me. For once they obeyed.

As soon as we were well clear, I quickly headed back to the house, opened up the gunroom and took out the .243, grabbed my sticks and binoculars from the utility room and shut the dogs in the kitchen. They were clearly disappointed that their walk had been cut short, but I had no time to explain to them at that moment the reason why. Jogging back around the edge of the farm, I slowed down well before I got to Five Bricks, for I did not want any potential shot to be thrown out of kilter by breathless panting on my part, and the final 200 metres along the grass margin were taken at the usual dead-slow stalker's pace.

When I got close to the point at which the muntjac had disappeared I scoured the grass with the binos and eventually picked up the tip of an ear where the buck had couched down in the grass. I imagine that after two

Left: A shot from the field margin

Below: A good December buck in the bag

and a half days of wet weather, he was enjoying the opportunity to dry off in a warm, south facing field margin. Luckily he was facing away from me, but now my task would be to get him to stand up so that I could see him, and yet not to spook him so severely that he might run without giving me a chance to shoot. Placing the rifle on the sticks, I gave a soft whistle. Nothing happened, so I whistled again, this time with more urgency, and at that the buck stood up. I shot instantly and he went straight down, a good half hour from when I had first seen him out of the barley. The dogs came and joined me outside once I had completed the gralloch, and I think that at last they understood – and appreciated – the reason for their hurried return to the kitchen.

The Valentine Buck

There are lots of different elements to a stalk: determining the whereabouts of the quarry by sound, scent and eventually at least by sight, good observation and fieldcraft, putting wind and weather to one's advantage, proficient marksmanship and, most of all, understanding the nature and habits of one's quarry. When it all comes together, it is highly rewarding, and it all came together for me one Valentine's day.

I guess that I am lucky in having a wife who not only loves field sports as I do, but who has a keen eye for spotting deer and is also a very competent rifle shot. To be fair, her real passion is hill stalking in Scotland and she leaves most of the low ground stuff to me, but once in a while she enjoys a sortie after fallow or muntjac and when I suggested that we might slip into something camouflaged on Valentine's morning, she agreed with surprising alacrity.

We had arrived well before daylight and stalked through one of my most productive woods without success so that by the time we got to the end of the wood, dawn was breaking. We turned to skirt the edge of the farm, and as we did so, a swirl of wind must have taken our scent deep into the brambles and blackthorn which line an ancient track on the boundary of the property. From out of the dense cover there came a single bark, followed by silence. The old buck knew we were there, but just as surely, he had given away his own position.

I thought for a moment, then whispered into Veronica's ear the suggestion that she should take a gentle walk along the track, thereby taking herself upwind of the brambles. Meanwhile, I crept slowly forwards to see if the muntjac might emerge. Perhaps he was aware that he was in danger of being outflanked, but for whatever reason, he avoided showing himself and for a while I thought all was lost until, some 300 metres ahead of me to the south, I just caught sight of a muntjac slipping through a fold in the ground into a small fir covert. It was the size of him which struck me, for he was obviously an old animal and even from that distance the white points of his antlers were easily picked out in the morning light. This was a beast of stature, certainly the largest I had seen on the farm for some while.

Veronica rejoined me after her excursion and I told her of my glimpse of the distant buck. There was little prospect of us catching up with him now, for he was well aware of the potential danger and clearly on the move through that fir covert. Together we glassed the field which spread out ahead of us, quiet and still in the cold, grey morning light, but as we did so, the unmistakeable figure of a muntjac emerged once more from top of the covert. It was the old buck, still moving steadily, but more slowly now, picking his way over the heavy plough, quartering away from us to the east. We dropped to the ground and watched him. Yes, there was no doubt that he was an impressive looking animal. He was evidently unaware of the fact that we were watching him and I fancied that there was just the hint of a limp in his steady gait.

By now he was almost at the far side of that ploughed field, some four hundred metres distant. In front of him was the field boundary, an old hedge. Many years ago it held an impressive stand of mature elms, but these have long since gone, and the spindly trees which sprouted up in their place have also died, leaving just a row of pale, bleached stems. At the back end of winter there was little cover in that hedge, as I well knew, but here and there was the occasional patch of bramble which offered a hiding place for deer, and I had surprised a roe or a muntjac there more than once in the past.

The buck turned and walked left-handed along the hedge. He was no more than a dot in the binoculars, silhouetted against the light as he crept along between the dead elms, going much more slowly now, but still on the move. My eyes were almost watering with the strain of trying to pick him out, but I could just about see the movement as he headed slowly along the field boundary until, beneath an ash tree with a broken crown, I lost him. There was a clear gap just a little further on, and I was certain he had not got that far. Evidently the buck had decided that he was again safe in the hedge bottom and had settled down once more. The stalk was on again.

Veronica and I both agreed exactly where we thought he was, and again I checked the wind direction. A light breeze had sprung up since dawn and it was quartering through the hedge in which the muntjac had stopped. Singlehanded, it would have been a difficult stalk, even an impossible one, for whichever side of the hedge I might have chosen to walk, the buck would have been sure to select the opposite one from which to make his escape. But this was Valentine's day, and I was not alone.

With great caution we made a big right-handed semi-circle across that field, hitting the hedge maybe three hundred metres from where the buck had stopped, whereupon I asked Veronica to walk slowly and quietly ahead of me on the upwind side, knowing that eventually the buck would wind her and

The Valentine Buck
– the product of
sporting teamwork

slip out of the opposite side of the hedge, directly in front of where I planned to be. Hopefully he would not do so too quickly and would offer the chance of a shot.

Carefully we proceeded down the hedge in this manner. It was a stalk which during the early part of the shooting season would have been impossible because of the number of game birds that would inevitably have announced our presence: even now the occasional pheasant erupted from the dead grass in the hedge bottom. But the hunting Gods were smiling upon us and eventually just 50 metres ahead I could see that ash tree, and to the right of it a little dip in the ground into which, I had a hunch, the buck would step.

The plan worked like a dream. The scent of a woman may be alluring to the human male, but to the muntjac buck it is just the opposite, and as he winded Veronica the old boy trotted out in front of me. I dropped to take a kneeling shot and whistled as I did so. He stopped. In that split second he must have known that he had made a fatal mistake, but by then it was too late: the bullet was already on its way. It caught him just below the shoulder and he lay still on the frosty ground.

In the exhilaration of the moment I was convinced that this battle-scarred old campaigner must be a gold medal. Ears torn, face cut and scarred from fighting and blind in his left eye, he had the longest antlers of any muntjac I had shot on that ground, and I decided at that moment to make a shoulder mount of him. The verdict was given five months later at the CLA Game Fair, where the CIC measuring team decided with regret that his brow tines were a tad too short to make gold, though they consoled me with a very satisfactory bronze gong. Perhaps I should have mounted him on a heart-shaped shield, but though I did not, he is nevertheless the embodiment of conjugal sporting teamwork as surely as if he had been shot with Cupid's arrow itself.

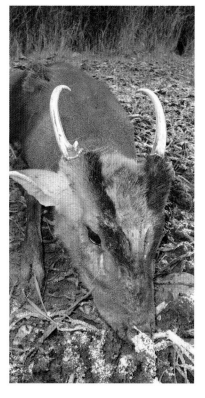

The battle-scarred old campaigner measured out at 56.3 CIC points – a bronze medal

Changing Fortunes

Muntjac stalking is capable of swinging the emotions of the hunter between extremes. Black despair at having repeatedly been made a total fool of by a crafty buck can quickly be followed by the exhilaration of a chance encounter and a shot well taken, while just as frequently the surge of adrenaline as an animal steps out at last light and the hunting genes kick in can be succeeded by that gut-wrenching realisation that while the beast may be down, it is not out, and there is a long and possibly fruitless search in prospect. This emotional see-saw can be no better encapsulated than in two successive outings which I made to a small farm near my home. The owner of the farm had asked me to deal with the muntjac that were troubling him.

It was Eastertide, and I had no more than got out of my land rover and walked past the farmhouse in the general direction of the portable high seat which I had erected for the occasion, than there was a skip and a jump out of the daffodils to my right and a muntjac doe departed. I cursed myself for being so careless and put the rifle on the sticks in case the doe should stop, which of course she did not, disappearing instead into a nearby hedge. The hour I spent in my high seat was fruitless, so I decided to go for a walk, and

Frosty morning – perfect for a stalk through the woods

as I checked the hedge bottoms around a small meadow with my glasses, there came a bark from just 25 metres away behind a thick bank of bushes.

How that animal winded me I don't know, for the air was completely still. But after a stand-off lasting five minutes, I was eventually treated to the sight of a white flag disappearing through the fresh cow parsley. It was almost as though the muntjac was taunting me with its defiance as it barked insolently from inside the wood where my high seat was located. The light was too far gone to take any further action that evening, but I was determined to get that animal.

So, the following morning I was up early and out in the frosty grass before daylight. This time I crept with huge caution towards my high seat, but as I passed an old orchard there came a bark to my left from the bottom of a hazel coppice some 50 metres away. That muntjac had again sensed that something was wrong, but although it was barking, it was obviously not yet on high alert. Slowly I sat down at the base of an apple tree and studied the coppice through my binoculars. Though it was barely light, I eventually saw the back of a muntjac doe moving about in the gloom. I raised the .243 and when I got an acceptable silhouette I squeezed the trigger.

There came no welcome thump of a strike, and the muntjac disappeared, so again I checked through the binoculars and eventually saw, against the early dawn, a muntjac standing on the far side of the coppice, looking quizzically in my direction. I could not get a clear shot through the brushwood and eventually it moved off, apparently quite uninjured. My heart sank in the belief that somehow I had managed to turn a useful stalk into a clean miss.

For the next hour I stalked this animal, up a hedge, into the meadow where I had spooked the muntjac the previous evening, then along the far side of the meadow where I saw it walking along a hedge line towards an old ash tree. But despite doubling back to approach the ash tree from downwind, I failed to pick it up. Once more the muntjac had beaten me.

After a walk around the farm on this beautiful spring morning I headed back to that hazel coppice for a final look and as I did so, I saw a muntjac just 100 metres beyond it, heading away from me. Once more the stalk was on, and once more this animal got the better of me, spotting me and making off down a hedge before I could pick it out amongst the fresh spring undergrowth. I could see that this was a buck and for a moment I thought I could get a shot at him as he passed through a gap in the hedge bottom, but this time there was no solid backstop behind him and I held my fire.

It had been a great morning's stalking, and the enjoyment which I had had in pitting my wits against these animals in the beautiful spring countryside had more than made up for my lack of success. But I had still not taken a proper look in that hazel coppice, which I had to pass once more on my way back to the land rover. When I finally made a quick search, it took me no more than a few moments to spot the doe lying dead where I had shot her some two hours earlier. The final swing of fortune had been in my favour. That doe which I had located in the half light had not been alone: there must have been a second animal just a few metres away from her which I had seen walking away after having taken my shot. It was evident that I had been stalking three different animals that morning.

8 CALLING ALL MUNTJAC

One of the alternative names by which muntjac were once known is 'barking deer'. Their sharp bark, like that of a small dog, can be heard through the woodland of southern England or echoing from hedgerow and thicket as they assert territorial rights, announce their presence one to another or alert all comers to the threat posed by a potential predator.

Communication by sound forms an important part of the life of what evolved for tens of thousands of years as a creature of the dense tropical and sub-tropical forest. It is also the cornerstone of a useful and fascinating strategy that can be employed by the muntjac stalker, for not only is it possible to call in muntjac to a static observer, whether he be armed with a rifle, a camera or even just a pair of binoculars, but it is also possible to stalk into a barking muntjac by sound alone.

Using a Call

The practice of calling quarry to a fixed hunting position is as old as hunting itself. German roe stalkers long ago elevated to a fine art the practice of calling roe bucks in the rut. Though the traditional tool is a beech leaf stretched between the thumbs of two cupped hands, a huge variety of artificial calls has been developed to imitate the sound of a roe doe in oestrus. Until relatively recently, however, few people realised that the same strategy – and indeed the same calls – could be used to entice muntjac towards a rifle.

I have known muntjac to be drawn to within just a few metres of a hidden observer with a series of squeaks from a blade of grass stretched, like that German beech leaf, between the thumbs. For consistency, however, a commercial call is better than natural products which are not always there when you want them, and by far the most popular, and probably the most successful call, is the Buttolo. This is a black, dome-shaped rubber bulb which, when squeezed lightly, emits a plaintive squeal. Buttolo calls are of course primarily designed for roe, so the vocabulary they are capable of imitating is

Calling with the Buttolo in the left hand, and ready to shoot off the sticks at a moment's notice. The call can be pushed into a jacket pocket to mute the sound

very extensive. Press the bulb sharply, for example, and you produce the 'rape' call of a roe doe being attended to by an over-amorous buck. For work with muntjac, however, we need to be gentle with our Buttolo, for it is that weak, plaintive squeal that is required to imitate the sound of a fawn in distress.

On only one occasion have I heard it for real, and it was quite distinctive. Stalking along the edge of one of my favourite muntjac woods in late spring, I heard the squeal come from deep in the cover to my left. It was a weak and rather pathetic sound, repeated half a dozen times with the space of about six seconds between squeals. Another stalker of my acquaintance has actually heard the sound being made by a young fawn as it was being handled. An adult muntjac is feisty in defence of its young, and we must presume that the intention of the call is to summon a nearby adult to assist in seeing off the danger.

It will of course be appreciated that there is an ethical question associated with calling in muntjac to a rifle by imitating a fawn in distress, for if indeed it is a doe which comes to investigate, then there is at least a strong presumption that she is doing so because she herself has a dependent fawn. Thus by shooting the doe, you are of course orphaning the fawn. While for those with a 'shoot on sight' policy geared to maximising the cull rather than achieving sustainable management this might not be an issue, for others it is.

For them, the answer is simple, and that is to avoid shooting any thin doe that responds to the call, remembering that where there is a doe, there will often be a buck not far behind.

The classic approach to calling muntjac is firstly to find a site in which an area of open woodland abuts dense cover where muntjac are known to be present and then to stand, with your back to a tree or dense bush that will break up your outline, on the edge of the more open woodland, facing the cover from which you hope to draw the muntjac. Wind direction is very important, and any breeze must of course be blowing from the direction you propose facing. Before showing itself, a muntjac is quite likely to attempt to get round behind you to catch your wind, so for that reason it is best to have your back close to the edge of the wood, since any approaching muntjac will be unwilling to leave the safety of cover and will thus have no option but to come at you from inside the wood.

Often there will be a buck not far behind

Sometimes a buck can be upon you within seconds

Before calling, set your rifle up on sticks and make sure you are absolutely ready to shoot at a moment's notice. The call can be worked with one hand, the volume being varied by squeezing it alternately from inside a pocket to mute the noise and then un-muted from outside the pocket. After a couple of calling sequences, stop, wait and watch very carefully, as an animal may appear out of absolutely nowhere. Perhaps there will be no reaction whatever, and often it will be several minutes before a muntjac arrives, but sometimes there will be a patter of leaves and a buck will be upon you within seconds. It is essential to remain absolutely motionless and perfectly camouflaged, because the animal will be looking directly at you and trying to work out what you are and what threat you pose. If a shot is to be taken, then the rifle must be brought to bear almost imperceptibly, whilst remembering that muntjac do not wait around for very long.

Often the best time to call is an hour or so after sunrise, towards the end of a morning stalk, but success may be achieved at any time of the day. On one occasion I was trying to make the best use of the 'down time' between morning and evening stalks during a two day group cull at the end of February. It was after lunch and I had elected to go out and try calling muntjac so, selecting a thick holly tree on the edge of a wood, I set up the rifle and waited, letting the wood quieten down completely before attempting to use the call. The first couple of calling sequences seemed to have no effect whatever, and after ten minutes the wood appeared totally dead. I tried a second bout of calling, and then a third, before waiting silently once more. It was only then, maybe half an hour later, that I realised that I was being watched by a young muntjac buck no more than 30 metres away. I had not seen him arrive, and the only thing that drew my attention to him was a shaft of afternoon sunlight shining through one of his translucent ears. With infinite caution I moved the rifle onto him, and he was in the bag.

It is, however, oh so easy to spook a muntjac that is looking intently at you, and equally difficult to spot it if it approaches through dense undergrowth. All you can do is to choose ground which gives you some advantage. It was early October and I had had a blank morning in the high seat when, walking quietly back towards the vehicle along a ride at the edge of the wood, I glanced to my left and saw the unmistakable hunchbacked shapes of a pair of muntjac moving through a coppice coupe. I saw them only for a couple of seconds, but as I suspected they had not seen me I decided that the best strategy would be to get to the downwind edge of the coupe and to use the call, with the open ride behind me. Choosing the best tree I could find as a background, I did just one calling sequence and waited. It was less than a minute before I saw just a slight movement in the undergrowth deep in front of me. Looking through the riflescope I was not able to pick out anything, so carefully I raised my binoculars and there, sure enough, was the head of a buck which was looking right at me. Now I was left with the conundrum of how to lower the binoculars and get my eye back to the riflescope without spooking the buck. Everything went well right up until the last moment, and I had him in the scope with my finger on the trigger when, with a bark, he ran off into the wood. It was a combination of errors: too much movement, perhaps an insufficiently good background and a foreground which afforded too much cover. You win some, you lose some.

Calling from a High Seat

But you do not have to be ground based in order to call muntjac successfully, for I have found that calling works very well from a high seat. It is not a strategy that I would wish to use often, certainly not from any of my regular high seat positions, because although I have no evidence to support this assertion I am nevertheless certain that it would be all too easy to end up with call-shy muntjac. But in a wood that is stalked only once in a blue moon, a calling session can at least offer another shot from the locker when a long wait in a high seat has failed to deliver the goods.

Occasionally the results can be quite dramatic. I had put up a portable high seat in an outlying wood on the estate. It was close to a release pen where I could see that there had been plenty of muntjac traffic, and I waited long into a cold February evening for a deer to walk out. Nothing had shown itself so, with maybe twenty minutes of light available, I got out the Buttolo and gave a couple of squeaks. Almost before I could put the call down there was a commotion to my left and a pair of muntjac appeared in front of me at about 25 metres. I dropped the buck on the spot, and the doe ran back into the wood, barking. The time from squeezing the call to taking the shot was under a minute.

A similar thing happened on another occasion when I was sitting in a seat that overlooked a ride. This time it was the doe that showed first, but

I could see that she was cautious and I could also see that she was thin. She stood for maybe two or three minutes barking from behind a coppice stool, and although I could have got a shot at her, I chose not to do so. It was lucky for me that I held my fire, for shortly afterwards a buck appeared from behind me and walked, bold as brass, across the ride, an act for which he paid the ultimate penalty.

Rarely is a buck so brazen. I recall another occasion in a high seat on a forestry estate where I was a guest. The seat was a tall one, set against a big, mature oak tree and, at last light after a blank evening, I decided to have a go with the Buttolo. Well, the result was instant. I heard the animal scampering up from behind me, whereupon it started barking. This continued for several minutes, but because the tree was at my back, I could not catch sight of the muntjac. However hard I tried to twist my body and peer round the trunk of that huge tree, the animal had the better of me. It was still there when the light went, and as I climbed down from the seat in the darkness it took one final bark and, with a crash of twigs and leaves, exited into the bushes beside me.

Tactical Calling

Calling does not have to be a set-piece affair. On the contrary, a call can be pressed into service on those many occasions when a muntjac has been detected in cover during the course of a stalk but remains out of sight. Provided that the animal has not seen you, or at least has not excessively been alarmed by your presence, then at the sound of a squeak its natural inquisitiveness will sometimes cause it to step out of cover for a few moments and offer the chance of a shot.

It was midsummer night's eve and to my right, a leaf-strewn bank sloped down towards a lake, its sparkling surface just visible through the trees. To my left, dense stands of nettles clothed the ground beneath the trees, obscuring virtually everything. Having been dropped off by my host at the start of an evening stalk, I had gone no more than 50 metres down the ride when, to my left, I caught the departing backside of a muntjac doe out of the corner of my eye. She had spotted me coming and was not going to wait around. But although she was obviously alarmed, the white flag was not fully raised and she was certainly not panicked, so I reached into my pocket for my Buttolo call and gave a squeak. The doe had stopped probably 90 metres back from the ride, and at the sound she barked at me. I squeaked again, and the doe barked repeatedly. Could I possibly call her back towards me, and if so, would I be able to spot her and establish whether or not she was a suitable target? It was worth a try and, with my rifle set up on my sticks, I worked gently with the call.

Suddenly there was another sound. From my right came the sharp bark of a second muntjac, a buck, which had been studying the goings-on from maybe 50 metres back in the dappled shade. With great care I raised my binoculars and just caught the tips of his ears moving about in the nettles. Good! Here was a much better opportunity, and slowly I moved the sticks through ninety degrees so that I could pick him up in my scope. There he was peering at me, his head moving from side to side in his curiosity, but although I could see bits of ear, eye and antler, there was no clear target to aim at. So, with my right hand steadying the rifle and my eye to the scope, I worked the Buttolo with my left hand and watched as the little buck barked back at me. The stand-off continued for maybe three minutes, and I was relieved that I had put on my head net and gloves – obviously the muntjac could see me, but equally it seemed that he did not know what I was.

The doe emerged at 40 metres to take a look

Now he was moving slowly through the undergrowth and, as he reappeared from behind the smooth, grey bole of a sycamore, I got a clear view of his shoulder. It was the work of a fleeting moment to squeeze off the trigger and at the report the young buck collapsed.

On another occasion I peered cautiously around the edge of a long ride towards the end of my morning's stalk, hoping that I might spot a deer out on the grass in front of me. I did so, but instead of being a comfortable 70 or 80 metres away, it was just 20 metres from the brambles through which I was looking. The doe had twigged that there was something not quite right, and with a couple of little hops she was into cover. I could see, however, that she was not in panic mode, so I waited a moment, knelt down and raised my rifle to cover the ride in front of me, then made a couple of squeaks on the Buttolo with my left hand. It was enough. The doe, which had retreated back into the undergrowth, emerged at 40 metres to take a look, and within a moment she was dead on the ground.

Stalking by Sound

Using a call to draw in muntjac is a fascinating art. I use it only sparingly, and prefer to do so in woods where I am not a regular visitor in order to avoid any risk of educating my local deer. But there is another stalking strategy that is even more exciting, in which it is the muntjac, not the stalker, which does the calling. It is not unusual to hear a muntjac barking repeatedly for many minutes at a time often, although not exclusively, early in the morning, an hour or so after it has got light. Just occasionally, when the wind is coming from the right quarter and when you know the geography of the wood sufficiently well to be able to pinpoint exactly where the barking animal is, it becomes possible to stalk in to a muntjac by sound alone.

I have achieved this only a few times over the course of my muntjac stalking career, once during March in a cold, desolate wood with a shifting wind in which I had constantly to change my angle of approach in order to avoid the buck catching a whiff of my scent. There was sufficient fallen timber to hide my approach and, when I finally caught sight of him, to provide cover for me to set up the sticks and raise my rifle to get a standing shot from about 60 metres. There was another time that I stalked in to a barking doe. It was late spring and the bluebells were out as I approached her through heavy cover,

Right: When you can pinpoint exactly where the barking animal is, it becomes possible to stalk in to a muntjac by sound alone

Below: I approached the doe through heavy cover

spotted her chestnut flank through the undergrowth and took the shot. As I did so, another succession of barks came from my right, but though I searched with my binoculars leaf by leaf for maybe half an hour, I never located what I imagine must have been the buck with which my doe was endeavouring to strike up a conversation.

However, my most memorable stalk by sound alone was on a grey morning in late April. It had started well with a shot at a young muntjac buck plucking his breakfast from the bramble bushes along the edge of a wood. I had already gralloched the deer, hung the carcass behind a field gate for collection later, and was just having a relaxing few moments cleaning my knife and folding shovel when, far off in the wood, I heard a high pitched bark, followed a few seconds later by a second bark, this time a lower pitched full-bodied one.

Again came the high pitched bark, and once more it was followed by the lower note. I stopped cleaning my spade and listened intently. It was as though a conversation was taking place between two different animals, and I realised that deep in the wood were two bucks engaged in some sort of territorial dispute. The wind was in my favour, so quickly I donned my jacket and face veil, both of which were lying on the ground where I had removed them to gralloch the young buck, slipped a round into the rifle and headed for the argument.

The two bucks kept up their barking and, having worked out in my mind roughly whereabouts in the wood they were, I was able to cover the first block of timber quite quickly, guided all the time by the conversation which was going on ahead of me. The wood is a regular stalking ground in which I know pretty well every track and deer path. The area from which the muntjac were barking was being used for game rearing. It comprised a feed ride and beyond it a large area of overgrown hazel coppice within which was situated a release pen. It was from the dense tangle of undergrowth below the hazel trees that the sound appeared to be coming.

So far I had made rapid progress, but I was not going to risk ruining the stalk by being over-hasty. The two muntjac were still barking at each other, and from the sound of their voices I could now start to estimate where each animal was located. Reaching the feed ride, I halted, checked right and left, and then proceeded with extreme caution towards the release pen, stopping every couple of metres or so to check ahead of me with the binoculars. It was painstaking progress, but I was by now able to establish almost to the square metre the position of each muntjac, and with every pace I refined my estimate.

One, the animal with the higher pitched voice which I took to be a young buck, was directly in front of me some 60 metres away, but in impenetrable cover. There was little hope of getting to him without ruining everything. If I were to take the best and quietest route to the older animal, a grass track around the release pen, I would have to pass no more than 30 metres from the youngster, but the slight breeze which filtered through the trees was still in my favour, and anyway, I knew that both animals had their minds on each other, not on the danger posed by an unseen stalker.

So, inch by inch, I crept past the young animal and headed for the more mature hazel where I knew the older buck to be. As I did so I hardly dared breathe for fear of breaking what was by now almost a magic spell, but my efforts paid off and some minutes later I reached my objective, a clump of brambles about 70 metres from the ancient hazel stools, their crowns already emerald green with young, fresh leaves. It seemed as though the older animal was patrolling in a small circle as he barked, and so with infinite care I set up my stalking sticks, placed my rifle on top of them and waited.

A painstaking stalk brought me up to the buck

For an age, it seemed that the barking continued directly in front of me. With my right hand holding my rifle, I levelled the binoculars and stared intently into the hazel coppice until, all at once, the buck came into view from behind a hazel stool, patrolling with his head down, barking once every few seconds. My eye moved from binoculars to riflescope. Smoothly I trained the reticle at a point just behind the animal's shoulder, eased off the safety and, moving the rifle gently with his forward gait, I fired.

He was in the hazel coppice just 70 metres ahead of me

At the sound of the shot, pigeons clappered out of the ash trees behind me and startled pheasants scarpered in squawking protest. The barking had stopped, but my eye was on the little window of green where I had last seen that muntjac. There, 70 metres away, among the vivid green stems of dog's mercury, lay a mature buck. He had the body of an old fighter, and what would have been a splendid head had not one of the finely curved tines been broken off, no doubt in some other territorial scrap. But the trophy is of importance only insofar as it is a reminder of an utterly enthralling stalk which I shall remember for a very long time to come, a stalk in which I was guided to the shot not by vision but by sound, the barking of a doughty old muntjac who defended his territory to the death.

9 A FEAST OF MUNTJAC

Even those who absolutely detest the muntjac for the impact which it may have upon their woods, farms or gardens will readily admit that the species has at least one virtue: it is extremely good to eat. In my own opinion, with the possible exception of the flesh of a young roe, muntjac venison is hard to beat.

The fine texture of the meat sets it aside from the venison that is derived from larger species, the flavour is invariably mild with a hint of the woods about it and there is never any of the harshness or rankness that is sometimes associated with the flesh of red stags or fallow bucks that have been taken during the rut. Moreover, the meat is usually very tender and succulent although, like all wild game, it must be treated correctly in the kitchen if that tenderness is to be transferred to the plate.

Because muntjac come in small packages, the carcass is easy to handle, and there is no need for the heavy lifting tackle which is required when the larger species are brought into the larder. But by the same token the game dealer is unlikely to be impressed by such a small beast. Muntjac are not easy to skin and they are fiddly and time-consuming to butcher, so in strict commercial terms the cost of preparation is barely worth the value of the meat, thus it is no surprise that the reward which one receives from the game dealer for muntjac carcasses is usually small. Indeed, some dealers will only accept them when they are accompanied by carcasses of other, larger species. These considerations are not necessarily an issue with the recreational stalker however, and since a muntjac takes up so little space in the domestic freezer, it is no surprise that a large number of animals are processed at home.

That at least is to the benefit of the true hunter, who can enjoy eating what he has shot without need to justify to himself or anyone else why it has not been sold to the game dealer. It does, however, mean that the wider public rarely gets the chance to eat muntjac, or at least to eat it in the full knowledge that it is muntjac that they are consuming rather than merely 'venison' in a burger or sausage. That is a real shame, though by the same token, those few specialist dealers who do make a point of marketing muntjac venison are to be greatly applauded.

Several years ago I ceased taking muntjac carcasses to the dealer and registered my own premises with my local authority for direct sales to the public. It is fascinating to meet the many customers who call specifically to buy muntjac venison and to discuss with them how the food they are buying has been shot in the wild and then processed and packaged. Some customers are in the area on holiday and are interested in taking home with them the authentic produce of my particular part of Suffolk. Others have had their gardens raided by muntjac and although they tell me that they want to experience the flavour of the beast, I secretly feel that most simply want to exact a form of revenge for the loss of their fruit and vegetables. Then there are those who are already converts, who have bought muntjac haunches or fillets in the past and discovered what a truly wonderful meat this is and who subsequently come back time and again for more, sometimes buying large quantities at a time in order to stock up their own freezers. Would that there were more such individuals, for if muntjac venison were to be fully recognised for what it is and marketed as such, rather than being minced, diced or added anonymously into burgers, then I truly believe that the status of the species would be improved. Furthermore, an increase in public demand for muntjac venison would help to press forward the national cull.

Driven by the resurgence of interest in fresh, local, natural produce, there is an increasing demand for wild venison, something which I find extremely refreshing. People are rightly interested in the provenance of what they eat. They want to enjoy food which comes from a particular locality or has been produced by an individual that they can identify with. This is a recurrent theme amongst those who turn up at my farm gate. However, while it is increasingly possible to buy genuinely wild, locally produced venison at small independent butchers' shops, the vast majority of it is branded simply as 'venison', and most of the meat will inevitably have been cut from red or fallow carcasses. Just as pork and beef is now successfully marketed as Gloucester Old Spot and Aberdeen Angus, the time is absolutely right for our wild venison to be marketed in a species-specific way and properly labelled as muntjac, roe, or even the increasingly widespread Chinese water deer. Only when this happens will the public recognise the worth of muntjac venison and appreciate the treat that they have been missing all these years.

Processing the Carcass

Primary preparation of carcasses is similar to that for other smaller species. Once the carcass has been field gralloched and brought into the larder with head and feet removed, it should preferably be hung in the skin. A chiller is a really worthwhile investment, for it means that several carcasses can be collected and held for preparation in a single batch when time allows. Furthermore, because muntjac carcasses are modest in size, a small chiller cabinet or game fridge is more than adequate. Five days at 7 ºC is usually about right, after which the carcass should be skinned and butchered. It must be said that skinning a muntjac is rather more difficult and time consuming than skinning a roe. The skin is thick, especially around the neck, and is not given up easily by its wearer. It may therefore be necessary to use the knife rather more than is the case with other species.

Left: When it has been brought to the larder, the head and feet are removed

Below: The carcass should be chilled down to 7 ºC and hung for around five days

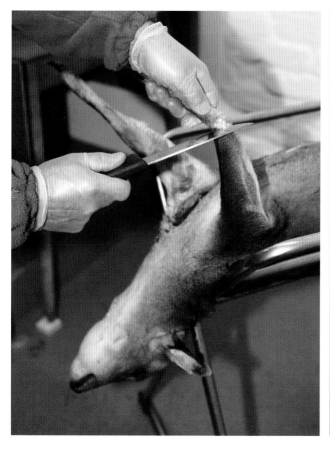

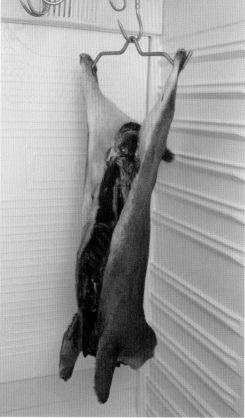

Muntjac do not give up
their skins easily, and it
will usually be necessary
to use the knife to a
greater extent than with
other species

A good muntjac carcass contains four different qualities of venison. Firstly there are the two haunches, which are best packed whole since they are too small to separate out into individual muscle groups. Carefully pare the haunch away from the pelvic bone, but leave the leg bones inside the joint. Then saw off the shank bone just below the knuckle joint and you will produce a neat and very presentable package for the freezer. The resulting haunches, which usually weigh from around 900g in a small animal up to 1250g in a good sized adult, make excellent roasting joints, suitable for a family of four or five.

Do not, however, discard the shanks, for if they are properly prepared, even these will make a superb slow-cook starter, as we shall see later.

Next there is the prime meat: the fillets or loins. These are best boned away from the carcass and the resulting strips of meat are absolutely delicious – succulent, sweet and with that fine-grained texture which is the hallmark of muntjac venison. One fillet strip off an average sized animal will serve two people comfortably, but after you have removed the fillets, don't forget to strip the tenderloins from the inside of the carcass. They will be found on each side of the spine, running from the rearmost rib back to the pelvis. They may only

be bite-sized, but they simply melt in the mouth. I have on occasions been asked to prepare a saddle of muntjac on the bone, which certainly makes an interesting and very presentable roasting joint, but I would regard this strategy as being appropriate for larger animals only.

The forequarter meat is best stripped from the bone, as the shoulders are not really worth treating as roasting joints. Diced muntjac forequarter, however, is perfect for casseroles and indeed for any recipe which calls for diced meat. And do make sure that the foreleg bones are retained for making stock.

Finally, the flank and rib flank, together with any meat stripped from the neck should be put through the mincer to make excellent mince for sausages, pasta sauces or stalker's pie – the venison version of shepherd's pie. Alternatively, if a neck is clean and undamaged, it may be slow cooked until the meat comes away from the bone. Any shot-damaged offcuts may be put in a casserole and cooked up as dog meat.

Rarely have I had a disappointing muntjac carcass. An old buck, though usefully sized, may demand a different butchering strategy, and if I shoot a

Above Left: The flank and rib flank, together with any meat stripped from the neck should be put through the mincer

Top Right: A muntjac prepared for the freezer: two haunches, two loin fillets, two packs of diced forequarter and a pack of mince

Above Right: Not forgetting the shanks, vacuum packed for freezing

really old stager, then I will strip the meat off the haunches and dice it for casseroles rather than roasting on the bone. The fillets of even an old muntjac are tender, provided that they are not overcooked, and those of a younger animal are simply heavenly.

The foregoing notes briefly summarise the preparation and butchering of a muntjac carcass. A fully detailed description of the processes involved may be found in my illustrated guide, *Practical Woodland Stalking*.

Cooking Muntjac Venison

As with all venison, and indeed all other game, the secret of preparing the prime cuts is to cook them hot and fast, a fact that has been lost on generations of British cooks. For so many people the first taste of venison has been from a haunch of red deer, possibly shot in the rut, slow roasted so that it emerges onto the plate a uniform grey in colour and tasting dry and unpalatable. It is not surprising that wild venison has had a hill to climb.

For all prime cuts that are to be grilled or roasted, use a really hot oven for a short period and then place the joint in a warming oven to rest. This completes the cooking process by allowing the muscle fibres time to relax and enabling the heat to migrate through the meat. As a rule of thumb, allow the meat to rest for a little less than half the cooking time and you will find that the outside will be nicely browned while the centre is still pink and succulent. It is a fallacy to suggest that venison is dry. This is only the case if it is cooked for too long. By following the 'hot and fast' rule, disappointment should be avoided. I place fillets on a high grill rack in a grill pan placed at the very top of the hottest oven in the Aga at the searing temperature of 240 ºC and flash them for ten minutes before resting. Likewise a haunch requires about 40 minutes. If you cook muntjac for too long then it will, as with every other species of venison, become uniformly tough and inedible.

Slow cooking cuts, on the other hand, should be brought to the boil and then allowed plenty of time in a gentle simmering oven surrounded by stock, wine or other suitable liquid so that any sinew within the muscles can slowly break down. Leave them to cook for several hours and they will be all the better for it. A casserole put into a low oven at lunchtime will be nicely ready for an evening meal at 7 p.m.

Accompaniments

Like other species of venison, muntjac may be complemented by flavours which reflect the woods and countryside from which it comes. A few strips of smoked bacon will augment the flavour of a roasting haunch, though contrary to popular belief it is unnecessary to add fat to a venison roast. Juniper berries are a favourite, as they convey the scent and flavour of pinewoods, and even better are those which you have collected yourself from juniper bushes in the forest or along the moorland edge. Fresh thyme and, especially, rosemary also provide that aromatic kick which lifts both a roast and a slow cooked dish or casserole. Likewise fruit jellies such as redcurrant or crab apple lend both a degree of sweetness and a note of astringency. A traditional accompaniment to game and venison, they work well both when added to a casserole whilst it is cooking and as an accompaniment at the table.

If you are serving up a home produced and locally sourced piece of meat, then there is a delightful synergy about accompanying it with home grown or at least locally grown vegetables. I accept that in my household we take this to extremes, and where some people calculate the food miles that are required to deliver their dinner to the table, we work in food metres. An ideal meal will thus comprise the meat from a deer shot on our own farm served up with vegetables from the kitchen garden. Great pains are taken to ensure that even the oils and flavourings that are used are as local as possible, so we are great supporters of Maldon sea salt which, if not of Suffolk origin, then at least comes from the neighbouring county. Locally grown and pressed rapeseed oil can replace Italian olive oil, juniper berries are collected on overseas hunting trips while, of course, fresh herbs come from the garden. There is even a very acceptable white wine that is grown just two miles away in a local vineyard and which can be brought up from the cellar when the occasion demands. We are still, however, wrestling with the problem of fresh black pepper, for unfortunately nobody yet has come up with an alternative which can be sourced from this corner of East Anglia. Nor does any English vineyard I can think of produce an acceptable red wine, though with luck and global warming that time may come in the not too distant future.

Muntjac Fillet Noisettes

This is my family's ultimate fast food. It is incredibly quick to prepare and when served with chips and peas – home grown of course – it makes an almost instant meal. Otherwise any fresh seasonal vegetables will suffice. One average sized muntjac fillet strip will feed 2 persons.

> *1 muntjac fillet*
> *1 teaspoon sea salt*
> *1 teaspoon mixed peppercorns*
> *A few juniper berries*
> *Olive oil*

1. Prepare the fillet by carefully removing all sinew and silver skin. Cut into two pieces.
2. Put the sea salt crystals, the peppercorns and juniper berries in a mortar and grind them coarsely by hand, then spread half of the mixture onto a work surface.
3. Roll one section of fillet in the mixture until it is well coated, then spread the remaining mixture on the work surface and do the same with the other fillet portion.
4. Place the fillet pieces on a grill pan, drizzle a little olive oil along its length and put into the top of a scorching oven (240 ºC) for 10 minutes.
5. Remove from the oven, allow to rest for about 3 minutes and then, using a sharp filleting knife, cut into noisettes onto pre-heated plates.
6. Serve immediately with home cooked chips and peas straight from the garden. To cheat, use oven chips and frozen petits pois.

Muntjac fillet noisettes with home-grown winter vegetables

Roast Muntjac Haunch

An average sized muntjac haunch makes an excellent family roast. Most prepared haunches will have little or no fat, so it is a good plan to cover the meat with rashers of streaky bacon. These will become crisp and are delicious to eat with the venison.

> *1 muntjac haunch*
> *2 or 3 good sized cloves of garlic*
> *Juniper berries*
> *Fresh rosemary*
> *Several rashers of streaky bacon*

1. Cut the garlic lengthways into thick slices. With a sharp pointed knife prepare the haunch by making short, deep cuts in the surface of the meat and into each cut insert a sliver of garlic.
2. Coarsely grind the juniper berries and rub into the surface of the prepared meat.
3. Place in a roasting pan, lay small sprigs of fresh rosemary on the meat and then cover it with rashers of streaky bacon.
4. Place in a hot oven (220 ºC) for 40 minutes.
5. Remove from the heat and let it rest for 15 minutes in a warming oven before serving.

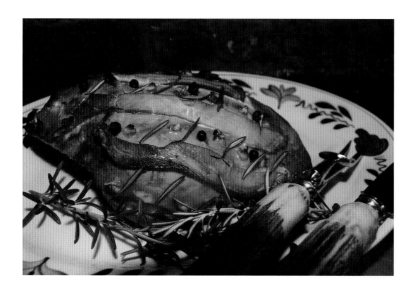

Roast muntjac haunch

Casseroles

Slow cooking is the best way to prepare the secondary cuts such as shoulder and forequarter. Venison casserole is a traditional favourite which is the perfect hearty meal for cold winter days. Although virtually any venison casserole recipe can be adapted for use with diced muntjac, this is a particular favourite which incorporates the flavours of orange and coriander.

Muntjac Casserole
with celery, walnuts, orange and coriander
(Serves 4-5)

1.5kg diced muntjac venison
2 medium onions
4 tablespoons of olive oil
2 sticks of celery chopped small
120g walnut pieces
Zest or finely cut peel of one orange
Juice of 1 orange
1 teaspoon of coriander seed
Large glass of red wine
150ml venison stock
Sea salt and freshly ground black pepper

1. Heat the olive oil in a casserole and add the chopped onion, stirring occasionally but cover with the casserole lid until the onions are caramelized and golden.
2. Add the diced muntjac, mix well and allow the meat to seal all over.
3. Add the chopped celery, walnuts and orange zest or peel.
4. With a pestle and mortar grind the coriander with sea salt together and stir them into the venison.
5. Add the orange juice, wine and stock and bring to a simmer.
6. Transfer the casserole to a simmering oven (120 ºC) or a slow cooker and cook for 4 hours.
7. Serve with rice or creamy mashed potatoes.

Liver and kidneys

Muntjac liver and kidneys are quite delicious. Always save them provided that they have not been damaged by the shot or otherwise. To avoid contaminating them in the field I normally leave them attached to the carcass during the gralloch, removing them later when I larder the carcass ready for the chiller. Ideally both liver and kidneys should be eaten fresh, and although they can be kept in a refrigerator for a couple of days, it is best not to leave them too long inside a carcass that is hanging in a chiller, as they will dry out. Alternatively they can be prepared and frozen for later consumption. It is best to put them in polystyrene trays and shrink-wrap them for the freezer.

Kidneys are at their best on the day that they are brought back to the larder. The ultimate place for them is as part of the stalker's breakfast, prepared late in the morning after a successful return from the woods. When we organise a group muntjac cull and have maybe six or seven stalkers around the breakfast table after a morning's stalking, a breakfast of scrambled eggs, locally cured Suffolk bacon, mushrooms, sausages and tomatoes is prepared in the Aga and served up on platters for everyone to help themselves. The muntjac kidneys, however, are reserved for the plates of those who have scored success that morning.

When preparing kidneys for breakfast, cut them in half lengthways, running a sharp knife gently through them until the two halves are held together only by the thin transparent membrane in which the kidney is encased. Then gently peel the membrane away from the kidney and place on top of the grill pan with your bacon for 5 or 6 minutes in a high oven. The longer you keep kidneys in the refrigerator, the more difficult it becomes to remove the membrane cleanly.

Below: A real stalker's breakfast of scrambled eggs, bacon and fresh muntjac kidneys

Bottom: Muntjac kidneys ready for the oven

Venison liver was formerly regarded as the perquisite of that most lowly member of the hunting team, the forester's knave, and throughout history liver more generally was despised as food for paupers. I remember the days during my childhood in rural Norfolk when my mother would struggle to get liver from our village butcher, as nobody wanted to have anything to do with it. Things are different now of course, and while all venison liver is good to eat, muntjac liver is particularly fine grained and quite delicate in flavour. In our household it is a regular standby, for when a muntjac comes into the larder the liver is quick to prepare and cook, and will make almost an instant meal long before the carcass itself has been skinned and butchered. Likewise a frozen muntjac liver will defrost within a few minutes and will feed 2 people.

Prepare it with tomatoes and onions. For a simple supper, rinse the liver and trim away any remnants of the diaphragm, then slice it into thin strips. Chop up a small onion and a clove of garlic and cook it on the hob in a shallow casserole until soft, then dust the liver with flour and brown it. Add a tin of chopped tomatoes and half a tube of tomato purée, season, cover the casserole and put it in a medium oven for 40 minutes.

For something a little more special, cook muntjac liver slowly with onions, red wine and, if you can get them, boletus, otherwise known as penny bun mushrooms, ceps or, in German, *steinpilz*. These have a flavour of the forest which is quite unlike that of field mushrooms. For perfect synergy, pick the mushrooms from the wood in which you have shot the muntjac. I learned to pick both boletus and chanterelles with my mother at the age of five and have done so in the same woods in Norfolk almost every year since. Fifty years ago, nobody else picked wild fungi in England, indeed, few people dared to do so for fear of poisoning themselves and their families. All that has now changed of course, and the woods are stripped bare each autumn weekend. However, it is still possible to find wild mushrooms if you choose your day carefully and know exactly where to search.

Liver, home-grown onions and boletus freshly picked from the woods

Muntjac Liver
with ceps and red onions
(Serves 4)

2 muntjac livers (approx 600g)
3 medium sized red onions
150g freshly-picked boletus (ceps)
2 glasses red wine
Plain flour
Olive oil
Sea salt and freshly ground black pepper
Fresh thyme

1. Peel and finely slice the onions, then fry them in the olive oil in a covered casserole until soft. Remove from the casserole and reserve.
2. Cut the livers into thin strips and dredge with flour.
3. Add a drop more olive oil to the casserole and brown the liver strips over a fast heat, then return the onions, add the red wine, turn down the heat and cover the casserole.
4. Prepare and dice the boletus and spread on the top of the bubbling contents of the casserole.
5. Add a couple of good sized sprigs of fresh thyme and season to taste.
6. Place the casserole in a low oven (110 ºC) for 2 hours.
7. Serve with creamed potatoes.

Muntjac liver with ceps and red onions, served with creamed potato

Heart

Even those who regularly eat venison kidneys and liver usually do not bother with the heart. Very often of course it is destroyed or at least badly damaged by the shot, and since it is the primary target this is hardly surprising. If my dog is with me, however, and particularly if she has found the

If the heart is undamaged, then be sure to save it

animal, I try to recover what remains of it. Such shreds of heart as still exist are then carefully pared away with my stalking knife and fed to her after the gralloch. Occasionally a muntjac is shot through the lungs or neck, and the heart is undamaged. In these cases I save it for human consumption.

By the time it is trimmed of all its appendages and hard tissue, a muntjac heart is not exactly large, and it would hardly make much of a main course unless a number of hearts were to be frozen and collected together. As a starter, though, a muntjac heart is perfect both in size, texture and flavour, especially when accompanied by the complementary flavour of bacon or pancetta and the texture of chopped nuts and mushrooms. For something quite exquisite, replace the button mushrooms with fresh chanterelles.

Muntjac heart with pancetta, sun dried tomatoes and Madeira

Muntjac Heart
with pancetta, sun dried tomatoes and Madeira
(Serves 2 as a starter)

1 muntjac heart
70g diced pancetta
1 shallot
Half a clove of garlic
6 button mushrooms
6 sun dried tomato pieces
Madeira
Olive oil
Sea salt and freshly ground black pepper
Walnuts, hazelnuts and almonds, about 25g in total,
chopped together

For the salad
Fresh salad leaves with rocket and chard
Olive oil
Balsamic vinegar
Sea salt and freshly ground black pepper

1. Prepare and dice the heart into small cubes. Peel and finely chop the shallot and garlic. Chop the tomatoes and cube the mushrooms.
2. Heat the olive oil on a fast hob in a small skillet until it is very hot, then toss in the shallot and garlic, the cubed heart and the pancetta.
3. Cook quickly and then add the mushroom cubes and the sun dried tomatoes.
4. When the heart has changed colour and the fat of the pancetta starts to melt, add the seasoning and a splash of Madeira and remove from the heat.
5. In two small serving dishes, create a green salad from the leaves, rocket and chard, and drizzle with olive oil (oil that is flavoured with orange is best if you can get it) and a few drops of balsamic vinegar.
6. Divide the cooked heart and pancetta mixture in two and place on top of the salad. Sprinkle with chopped nuts.

Shanks

Removing the shank from a muntjac haunch makes the joint a much neater package for the freezer, but until a few years ago I used to do little with the shanks themselves, either stripping the meat off for mincing, or simply tossing them in the pot of offcuts destined for the dogs. That was before I realised how delicious they were. A muntjac shank may be small in size, but when slow cooked in the manner of a lamb shank, it makes a really mouthwatering bite. Two shanks produce a really unusual starter, and four shanks, served with creamed potato, are a substantial enough main course to satisfy the keenest appetite.

Braised Muntjac Shanks
(Serves 8)

16 trimmed muntjac shanks
2 medium sized onions
1 clove of garlic
Olive oil
300ml venison stock
2 or 3 sticks of celery
Glass of white wine
Rosemary
Bay leaves
Mixed peppercorns
Sea salt

1. Finely slice the onions and sweat them in a covered pan with the chopped garlic in a little olive oil until they are soft and transparent. Remove them from the pan and set them aside.
2. Add a dash more olive oil to the pan and quickly seal the shanks in batches.
3. Take a large, shallow casserole, put the cooked onions and garlic in the bottom, then arrange the shanks in the bottom of the casserole, filling any remaining spaces with short pieces of celery.
4. Pour on the stock, then with the white wine deglaze the pan in which you fried the onions, adding the liquid to the casserole so that all the shanks are sitting in the liquid without being fully covered by it.

5. Place a few sprigs of rosemary and bay leaves on top of the shanks, sprinkle on half a teaspoon of mixed peppercorns and a generous pinch of sea salt.
6. Place the casserole on the hob until it starts to simmer, then remove to a simmering oven (110 ºC), cover and cook for four hours.

I find this dish works very well when cooked in an old fashioned cast iron pan, covered with aluminium foil. Serve as a starter, 2 shanks per serving, with a spoonful of the onion and stock, and a knob of redcurrant or crab apple jelly.

Braised muntjac shanks

Stock

Good venison stock is the foundation of so much game cookery. Meat for slow cooking should be simmered gently in stock, while it can be added to casseroles and stews to prevent the meat from drying out and catching at the bottom of the pan. In addition, good, flavoursome stock is the ideal basis for a wide variety of soups. It is terribly easy to make, provided that you retain sufficient venison bones whilst butchering a carcass. Muntjac bones are ideal, and I find it easiest to retain for stock-making the bones from the forelegs once they have been stripped of meat. It is important to crack the long bones, which is easy to do with a meat cleaver, as this allows the bone marrow to melt and infuse into the stock. Ideally, make your stock shortly after butchering a carcass, but if this is not possible, then bones may be frozen for processing at a later date.

Muntjac Stock

All the bones from 4 forelegs that have been stripped of meat
1 large onion
2 bay leaves
6 cloves
3 sticks of celery
3 carrots
1 teaspoonful of crushed mixed peppercorns
4 pints of cold water

1. Break all the long bones from the forelegs. If they are simply chopped in half then they will fit easily in a large casserole or stock pot.
2. Roughly chop the onion, celery and carrots, add the other ingredients and cover with the cold water.
3. Bring to the boil, place in a low simmering oven (110 °C) and leave overnight.
4. When the stock is cooked, allow to cool and then pour through a sieve into suitable storage containers and freeze for future use.

One litre ice cream tubs are highly suitable for freezing stock. However, an alternative if you have the space is to freeze in yoghurt pots. This enables you to thaw and use small quantities without having to thaw an entire tub or attack a large chunk of frozen stock with a saw.

Simple Suppers

Venison cookery is not all about fine dining. Diced or minced venison is the basis for a whole range of staple meals, and when the freezer is full of it, nothing is easier than to grab a pack of muntjac mince with which to prepare a quick supper at the end of a busy day. One of the most basic and most delicious offerings is a Bolognese sauce, which can be made from start to finish within 45 minutes.

Quick Muntjac Bolognese
(Serves 2-3)

500g muntjac mince
1 medium onion
1 clove of garlic
1 can of chopped tomatoes
1 glass of red wine
Half a tube (or a small can) of tomato paste
Olive oil
Salt and freshly ground black pepper

1. Finely chop the onion and garlic, and fry in the bottom of a shallow casserole pan until soft and translucent.
2. Add the mince (if this is straight from the freezer then defrost it first in a microwave). Quickly brown the mince all over, then stir in the tomatoes, tomato paste, red wine and seasoning.
3. Bring to the boil and then place in a hot oven (180 ºC) for half an hour and serve with spaghetti.

10 TROPHIES

unters have always been fascinated by antlers. Antlers have been associated with folk ritual the world over since the earliest times, while their display on the walls of a medieval hall would have demonstrated the hunting prowess of its owner for all to see. Thus it is no surprise that the collection, preparation and assessment of trophy antlers has become an integral part of the culture of deer stalking as the sport has developed down the years. Trophies have an aesthetic quality in their own right, and when displayed in the hunter's home they are a permanent reminder of days spent on the hill or in the woods. They have a practical value too, for with species such as roe deer, detailed records of the changing quality of trophy heads can be a valuable aid to long term sustainable management. That is not, at least not yet, the case with muntjac, where the objective of most landowners is to reduce numbers so far as is possible or at the very least to maintain an adequate cull. Even those estates which sell the occasional trophy muntjac regard such animals more as a bonus which comes as part of the overall cull rather than as an asset to be cultivated and nurtured alongside the quality roebucks or red stags.

Even so, things are changing fast and muntjac trophies, in common with deer trophies of all species, are becoming increasingly sought after as stalking itself increases in popularity. Whereas not many years ago the average muntjac carcass was fed to the dogs and the antlered head disposed of along with the bones or left to rot down in a dung heap, today, thanks at least in part to the wealth of stalking books, magazines and websites, a good quality head is much more likely to be recognised for what it is, appreciated and prized. Furthermore, since the trophy culture is stronger in continental Europe and the USA than it is in Britain, there is growing interest from overseas hunters in making a visit to England, the only country outside south east Asia with a significant muntjac population, in order to add a muntjac buck to their collection.

For the British stalker, the opportunity to take a really exceptional muntjac trophy is no less exciting, while even the collection by regular muntjac shooters of less significant heads can shed fascinating light upon antler morphology.

Preparing a Trophy Head

Trophy preparation should be considered from the moment a suitable buck is shot, for if an exceptional animal is being looked at as a potential shoulder mount, then it is essential that it is gralloched with care. Any knife work to the neck or throat must be avoided, for the resulting damage to the skin will be almost impossible for even the most skilled taxidermist to repair and will affect the finished mount. Trophies for shoulder mounting should be caped forwards of a line taken from behind the forelegs up to the centre of the back, thus providing the taxidermist with the maximum possible amount of material to work with. There is many a stalker who has blithely proceeded with his regular field gralloch only to regret bitterly having done so when he has got the carcass home and realised that he has a substantial medal head on his hands.

If a conventional skull mount is all that is required, then of course the head can be removed at the larder as usual, after which it should be skinned and prepared as soon as possible after shooting. If a head is left, even in a chiller, for days or weeks before it is dealt with, then it is likely that the finished result will appear discoloured. Some stalkers like to prepare and display the whole skull minus the lower jaws but including the tusks. More usual, however, is the preparation of a frontlet consisting of the top portion of the skull, the pedicles and the antlers.

Carefully skin the head. It is easiest to start from the nose, working from the jaw line upwards along the front of the face, before freeing the skin around the back of the skull. Particular care must be paid to the pedicles, and it will usually be necessary to cut the skin firstly between the antlers across the crown of the head and then pare it gently away, working up each pedicle to the coronets.

Once the head is fully skinned, it can be cut. The style of cut is very much down to the stalker's own preference, but the most usual cut is made from the back of the skull through to the mid point of the face on a line which

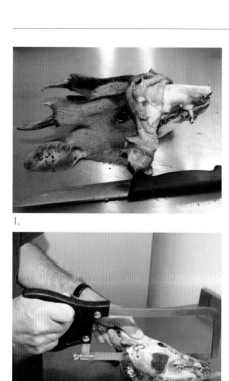

1.

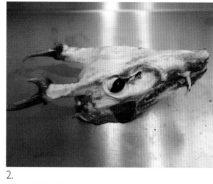

2.

Trophy Preparation

1. Remove the head and skin it as soon as possible after shooting

2. The head fully skinned

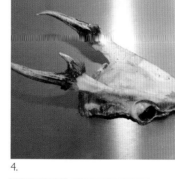

3.

4.

3. With a butcher's saw, cut the skull to your preferred size. A cut through the bottom third of the eye sockets makes a good frontlet trophy

4. The cut head. Don't forget to save the tusks, if required, before discarding what remains of the skull

5.

6.

5. Boil the trophy until the facial cartilage starts to separate from the bone

6. Scrape all tissue away from the skull with a short bladed kitchen knife

7.

8.

7. Cut away the fine nasal bones from the inside of the skull

8. With a kitchen scouring pad, rub the skull all over to remove any traces of soft tissue from the bone

runs from the ear canals through the bottom third of the eye sockets. The lower half of the skull is of course discarded, but do not forget to remove the tusks if these are to be retained either as part of a trophy mount or for some other purpose. Prise them carefully out of the jaw with a strong blade.

Place the cut skull in a pan and cover it with boiling water up to the coronets, then bring back to the boil. If you have saved the tusks then these too may be added to the boiling pan. Most muntjac trophies require around 20 minutes of boiling, but an old animal may require half an hour or more. Boiling can be a decidedly smelly procedure, and is best done either over a gas stove in an outbuilding or when your better half is out of the kitchen for an extended period. When the facial cartilage starts to separate from the skull, then the trophy may be removed from the pan, the eyeballs extracted from the sockets and the brain removed from the cranium. With a short bladed knife, then scrape all the tissue from the skull, leaving it absolutely clean. Pay special attention to the rubbery, gelatinous material below the coronets. When you have removed all the tissue from the outside of the skull and the pedicles, turn the trophy over and carefully cut away and remove the fine nasal bones from the inside of the skull, cleaning and washing it as you do so. Finally, take a kitchen scouring pad and rub the skull all over to remove any last traces of soft tissue from the bone. Then set the trophy aside to dry, making sure that it is well out of the reach of any dogs, which for some reason are unable to distinguish between a valuable sporting trophy and a tasty bone. Your dog will, however, be delighted to polish off the brain plus any scrapings you might care to give him.

Don't forget to remove the tusks from the pan. These can easily be cleaned off with the scouring pad, but in all except the oldest animals you will need to use a toothpick to remove the core of dark tissue from the centre of the tusks. If this is done carefully, then the core should come out in one piece.

Trophies may be mounted on a suitable shield for display, perhaps with the tusks glued underneath. Alternatively, if they are being kept for record purposes, they can be fixed in date order to a suitable piece of timber. I prepare and keep all the bucks I shoot, of whatever size, and it is very interesting to see the slight variations in antler form and set, and to observe them recurring in the same woods in successive years.

Oddities

Occasionally odd-shaped heads turn up. Always of interest to the stalker, these are often associated with disease or injury, perhaps sustained at the time when the antlers were growing. Sometimes a kink in the pedicle will betray the fact that the buck has sustained an accident, and antlers with broken pedicles occasionally produce a misshaped knob or lump instead of a conventional point. On other occasions a lack of symmetry in the antler formation suggests injury elsewhere in the animal. Deer of all species that suffer leg or foot injuries which result in a limp will tend to grow a misshapen antler, often on the side opposite to that which bears the injury, and this is as true in muntjac as in red deer although the results are perhaps less obvious.

Left: Malformed antlers caused by damage to the pedicles during antler growth. The healed fracture to the left pedicle can be seen, and the left antler has developed into an unusual castellated bony mass

Right: Malformation due to leg injury. An old injury to the nearside hind leg has caused this animal to limp during the period of antler development

Malformation due to hoof overgrowth. The third digit of the nearside hind foot has fractured, the second digit is missing completely and the joint between the digits and the cannon bone has fused, resulting in the hoof curling upwards so that it has almost formed a hook. The nearside leg is nearly 2cm shorter than the offside, and the resulting limp during the period of antler development has resulted in the right antler being considerably shorter than the left

Rather more spectacular is the multi-pointed head, such as the six pointer shot in 2012 in Berkshire. While this is the only one of its kind on record, it is quite likely that there are other similar animals out there waiting to be discovered.

Trophy Measuring

A good representative head with nicely curved main beams and two brow tines will delight most stalkers, particularly those who have never before shot a muntjac buck. However, there may come an occasion when a potential medal trophy is worth taking to an official measurer. A number of different formulae are used to measure hunting trophies worldwide, while at home in Britain, BASC offers its own measuring service to UK stalkers. Even so, if a stalker wishes to have his trophy measured according to an internationally recognised benchmark, then it is most probable that he will go to a measurer accredited by the International Council for Game and Wildlife Conservation (CIC), a worldwide advisory body based in Hungary which aims to preserve wild game and hunting. The measurer will carefully determine the precise dimensions of the trophy according to a set procedure, and will award it a number of points. This score will then be used to determine the quality of the trophy and whether it achieves bronze, silver or gold standard.

A spectacular 6 point muntjac shot by A Bingley, Berkshire, and measuring 77.2 CIC points

INTERNATIONAL COUNCIL FOR GAME AND WILDLIFE CONSERVATION

CERTIFICATE OF MEASUREMENT
Muntjac Buck

Owner's Name ....   Date Shot...............................

Approximate Age...........................   Locality ....

Number of Tines (left)		Number of Tines (right)	
Tip to Tip	cm	Greatest Spread	cm

SCORE DATA	A	B	C	D
	Span Credit (cm)	Left (cm)	Right (cm)	Difference (cm)
1. Inside Span between Main Beams				
2. Length of Main Beam				
3. Length of Brow Tine				
4. Circumference of Coronet				
5. Circumference of Antler at mid-distance up beam				
6. Column Totals				
	Add A+B+C	Subtract D=	**FINAL SCORE**	

MEDAL AWARD LEVELS

Bronze 56   **Silver 58.5**   **Gold 61**

Date........................   Signed ....

United Kingdom National Permanent Trophy Commission

Copyright © CIC 2009

The CIC certificate of measurement for a muntjac buck

For a muntjac to be in with a chance of a CIC medal, each main beam will usually need to be at least 10cm in length, measured from the underside of the coronet right the way to the antler tip around the outside of the antler, and there will need to be brow tines of at least 1cm on both sides. Brow tines are measured from the upper side of the coronet and it should be noted that tines measuring less than 1cm do not count at all. Thus a brow tine of 9mm will score zero. The circumference around the coronets should measure at least 8cm. Quite often this circumference is angled and therefore difficult to measure, so the measurer will use a piece of masking tape to follow around the edge before spreading the tape out on a table top and measuring it. At the mid point of the beam, the antlers should have a circumference of about 4cm and the span between the antlers should be around 11cm. Symmetry is very important, with any unevenness between the two antlers resulting in deductions being made from the overall score.

Any potential medal trophy is worth taking to an official measurer for formal assessment

Three gold medals. All three trophies achieved similar scores even though they are very different. The left hand trophy (63.1) has been scored down because it is very narrow; the middle trophy (63.3) although apparently unexceptional, has antlers that are much more widely set and even with a broken point achieves a high score because of the width of the span; the right hand trophy (63.7) has neither the span nor the symmetry, but has long brow points and great thickness of antler

There are no additional points for colour or beauty as is the case with trophies of some other deer species, and the skull cut is irrelevant. Furthermore the weight or mass of antler is of no consequence to the score, so the trophy does not need to be dried for any particular length of time and may therefore be measured freshly prepared. All that is required for a muntjac trophy to be accepted for measurement is that the antlers must be naturally affixed to the pedicles. They must not have been broken and reattached. Shoulder mounts as well as skull mounts may be measured, provided that the measurer is confident that the taxidermist has not altered the set of the pedicles.

Because a muntjac head is small in comparison to trophies of other species, even minute variations in measurement can count for a great deal, often making the difference between a good representative head and a medal. This also means that alive and on the hoof it is hard to distinguish a medal head from a run-of-the-mill decent buck or to determine the finer points of antler quality in the field. While you may, for example, get a good indication that a buck has a good length of antler, it is difficult to gauge the extent to

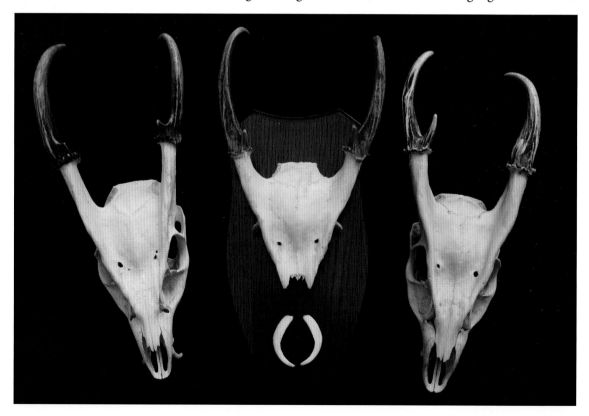

Left: Two first heads that show dramatic difference in pedicle set. The left hand buck could potentially have gone on to make an excellent trophy, while the narrow set of the pedicles on the right hand buck mean that it would never have produced a high scoring head

Below: A very attractive head, but only a silver medal. Both antlers taper away quite rapidly and the antler circumference at mid-distance up the beam is insufficient to achieve the required CIC points

which the antler tips of an old animal curl over, and it is virtually impossible for even a skilled professional stalker with a spotting scope to pick out the brow tines on a buck. The only aspect of a trophy which can reasonably be assessed through binoculars or telescope is the set of the pedicles. Some bucks have relatively closely set, parallel pedicles whereas others have pedicles with a significant angle of spread. Naturally it is the latter which will have the greater span and which will thus score more highly as trophies. As a result, those professional estate stalkers who do manage muntjac bucks for trophy clients will tend to spare the younger bucks with widely set pedicles, as it is these animals which will make the better trophies when they are mature.

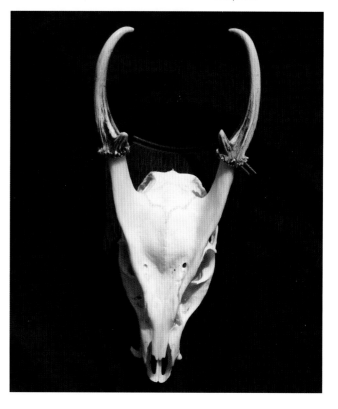

The current UK record muntjac, shot in Buckinghamshire and scoring 79.9 CIC points, was exhibited at the CLA Game Fair in 2009

If a trophy appears to be in the running for a medal, then it is well worth taking it to an accredited measurer. The BASC service may be contacted through the Deer department at the association's headquarters. CIC measurers attend the principal game fairs and the CIC team will always be found at the

British Deer Society stand at the annual CLA Game Fair. There are eight CIC measurers in the UK, of which five are in England. Alternatively you can visit a measurer at home or send your trophy to him through the post.

To achieve bronze medal standard under the CIC system, a trophy must reach at least 56 points. A trophy of 58.5 will achieve silver and one of 61 points or more will make gold. Year on year, there is an increasing number of trophies of all sorts coming forward for measurement, and it is therefore not surprising that the number of really good quality bucks on record continues to creep upwards. Currently the UK record is a buck shot by Mr J Harding in Buckinghamshire, with main beam lengths of 17.4cm (L) and 17.5cm (R); brow tine lengths of 2.3cm (L) and 1.9cm (R); and a span of 12.7cm; totalling 79.9 CIC points.

This animal was spotted in an Austrian gun shop. To many Europeans the muntjac is a highly desirable exotic species

Trophy Shooting Opportunity

Demand for good quality trophies is significant, with many visiting hunters coming from Germany, Holland, Denmark, Spain and the USA. Since England has such a unique range of introduced exotic species, visitors are often looking for muntjac and Chinese water deer in one trip, and so those estates in the south and east of England which can offer both species are at a distinct advantage. As the market for trophy muntjac grows, both individual estates and hunting outfitters are actively promoting muntjac stalking at international fairs in Germany and the US, while the growth of hunting communities on *Facebook, Yeswehunt* and other social media, serves to spread the word about muntjac stalking ever more widely.

On stalking estates where trophy muntjac are actively marketed, there will often be a policy of shooting all yearling bucks that are seen, but of leaving those with modest antlers, especially those which are widely set, as they will in due course improve in quality and may potentially be sold as a trophy. Trophy

The author with a happy team of hunters from Belgium and Germany after two successful days hunting on an estate in Essex. Muntjac are greatly prized by sportsmen visiting from overseas

size generally increases with age, so the estate which conserves its older bucks for trophy clients is rewarded accordingly. In very old bucks, however, the trophy may 'go back' with one antler becoming shorter and making the head appear lopsided. When a trophy buck is spotted, its location may be noted and, because the species is territorial, an observant stalking guide will perhaps be able to return later with a paying guest in a high seat or ground hide and wait until the animal shows itself once more.

As a result of its steadily expanding range, there are considerably more estates and outfitters offering muntjac stalking in Britain today than compared even to a decade ago, and thus prices may vary considerably. However, hunters visiting from overseas will often go to the principal estates where muntjac have been a regular item on the menu for some years, and can expect to pay from £400 for a good trophy up to £550 for a really substantial one, with most estates basing their charges on antler length. Often a basic outing fee is payable in addition, with clients stalking for two or three days in order to guarantee their trophy buck. Cull stalking prices are substantially less than this of course, with estates generally charging around £200 per day, often to UK stalkers. On an estate or property with a significant muntjac population and the stalking infrastructure to support visiting clients, stalking revenue can be significant, and that must surely be to the good for those estates which can reap the rewards. But it must also be good for the muntjac too, for it lends a commercial value to a creature which formerly had none. And that may in turn help to improve the management and welfare of the species, for a resource which is not valued commercially is all too often disrespected and abused.

Muntjac Art and Artefacts

The image of the deer's head and its antlers is an iconic motif that is fully embedded in the mainstream of art and design. There is of course a long history of game trophies being used to decorate country houses and hotels, but it seems that in recent years deer heads have actually become increasingly popular as wall decorations, as witness the miniature multicoloured decorative stags' heads which can now be seen in almost every home furnishing shop or which can be ordered online from the better class of department store. Genuine trophy heads, whether shoulder mounts or frontlets, are in a world

The deer motif features strongly in a wide range of giftware and decorative objects, especially at Christmas. Now among them is a depiction of a muntjac. Not exactly a lifelike muntjac, but a pioneer one nonetheless

of their own. Today they fetch substantial sums at auction, where they are snapped up more by interior designers than by hunters and collectors.

Despite this, relative to other deer species, muntjac barely feature in those many arenas where deer interact with humankind either on an aesthetic or practical level. They may have been present in Britain for over a century, but they have yet to register in any meaningful way with our culture, and neither do their products – other than venison and trophies – have any significant value. I have yet to see muntjac antler lovingly carved or worked in the way that roe antler is in Germany, or transformed into objets d'art like the candlesticks or other decorative items that are often made from the antlers of red deer. It grieves me each time I have to dispose of a muntjac skin. There is no commercial market for them and though I have cured and tanned them myself for rugs, they are difficult and time consuming to prepare, and barely worth the trouble.

Things may yet change, however. Recently I received as a gift a decorated tin, a simple container that could so easily have pictured the more traditional red deer or indeed any other wildlife motif. But it did not – it pictured a muntjac, or at least somebody's impression of one. The image is not exactly lifelike, but it is a start. I use the tin to store prepared muntjac tusks.

Fly Tying

Muntjac hair is of interest to the salmon or trout angler who ties his own flies. The hair from a muntjac's tail is particularly useful, and I have a local commercial fly manufacturer who eagerly takes muntjac tails from me. Because it is fine in comparison to the fly tyer's regular fodder of red deer hair, it is useful both for making wings and even for the dubbing which may be used to coat the thread wound onto the shank of a hook in order to build up the body of a fishing fly. The long chestnut-coloured hair from the upper surface of a muntjac's tail in summer is particularly suitable for trout flies, as it can be used to replicate many invertebrate species.

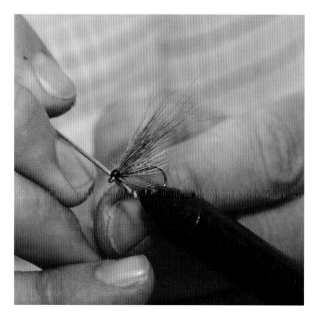

Above: A trout fly tied from the tail hair of a summer muntjac doe

Left: Muntjac hair is of value to the fly tyer

then kicking right and left as appropriate. In order that this could be done without damaging the tusks, and because the tusks of immature animals have an open root, they first had to be filled with a clear resin. Rather than risking damage to the precious tusks which had been selected, Jackie experimented on a few spare tusks to ensure that the resin would not alter the colour and, when she was satisfied, she went ahead with the resin fill, then trimmed and polished the tops before arranging for a specialist craftsman to undertake the drilling. She then strung the necklace, completing the design with a few bone beads and a silver clasp.

The result is simply stunning. While it has, as expected, something of an ethnic feel about it, the necklace, with its froth of white upturned points, when looked at from a distance appears almost like lace. In its black presentation case it certainly made a 'wow' as a wedding anniversary present to my wife.

It also made something of an impression during its first outing at the British Deer Society's 50th Anniversary gala dinner, appropriately held at Woburn, the spiritual home of muntjac in Britain. At present, I believe the necklace to be unique, at least in this country. However, more than one stalker's wife has given it an admiring glance, and it seems not unlikely that other muntjac stalkers are even now busily collecting tusks. I can assure them that, however industrious they might be, it will be some years before they will be ready to give the result of their labours to their loved ones, although I can equally guarantee that the moment, when it comes, will be worth the wait.

Painting and Sculpture

Deer have been a subject for painters and sculptors for at least 15,000 years, when our hunter ancestors drew their designs in charcoal and ochre on the cave walls at Lascaux. They run as a constant theme through British art, from Stubbs to Landseer and from Millais to Lionel Edwards. Not surprisingly, none of these eminent animal artists painted muntjac and only Edwards, who died in 1966, would have been at all likely even to see one. Despite the introduction of three new species and the welcome return of the native roe to so much of England, sporting art as it appertains to deer has, for the last century, been locked firmly in the highlands. Granted, the spectacular scenery of the Scottish hill and the grandeur of the red deer which inhabit it combine to conjure up a powerful draw to the artist, a draw that is enhanced by the clinking of coinage in the pockets of his wealthier sporting clientele, who have usually been brought up on a diet of hill stalking.

But perhaps things are changing. Roe deer appear regularly in exhibitions of sporting and wildlife art, and now for the first time we are starting to see the appearance of muntjac. The 'red spot' group of painters who exhibit each year at the CLA Game Fair have produced a number of striking muntjac pictures, some of the most exquisite being the work of Keith Sykes, whose scraperboard studies are quite breathtaking. The picture which he exhibited in 2013 really captures the presence of a muntjac buck. One can sense the alertness of this animal and almost feel the softness of the hair around the tops of his pedicles.

Muntjac
Scraperboard by
Keith Sykes

Muntjac
Oil by
Rodger McPhail

Another painting which deserves recognition is a masterly work by Rodger McPhail, for thirty years at the forefront of British sporting art. Rodger's animals and birds have the spark of realism in them that is the mark of a painter who knows and understands intimately the creatures which he is depicting on canvas, and his study of a muntjac buck stepping out of cover into a woodland clearing in late winter is the best I have seen. He has caught perfectly the confidence of a mature buck emerging onto one of his regular paths to patrol his territory. Determined and alert, this chap knows where he is going and is not going to hesitate and look around him. The bare, dank woodland floor is dimly lit, and evening is drawing in: it is a scene I have witnessed on hundreds of occasions, whether from a high

Left: Glass engraver David Whyman at work

Below: David Whyman's muntjac is the work of an artist who knows his subject from life

seat or when stalking on foot, and it is one which gives me that momentary surge of adrenaline each time I look at it. The quintessential muntjac stalker's picture by one of our finest sporting artists.

Slowly we are seeing more of muntjac in art, as painters, engravers and sculptors start to appreciate the species and its unique character. The glass engraving of David Whyman deserves mention, and it was a delight to be able to buy a greetings card recently at my local gift shop depicting a buck standing silhouetted in a winter field.

Above: *Field Visitor*
Linocut by
Rob Barnes

Right: Muntjac sculpture.
Teak root carved by
an unknown artist in
East Timor

Rob Barnes's linocut shows the unmistakeable outline of a muntjac alone at dusk in the East Anglian landscape amongst the sweeping furrows, the bare hedgerow trees and, in the foreground, the skeletal stems of last summer's cow parsley. It is the image of an animal which is at home in its environment, now firmly embedded amongst our local fauna.

But perhaps the last word should go to the unknown artist from East Timor whose sculpted muntjac swirl around a teak root which I spotted amongst the wares of a company offering for sale imported garden ornaments. They flow, like deer slipping and weaving through the undergrowth beneath their native tropical forest. They look like muntjac, they feel and behave like muntjac, they have that indefinable essence that is the product of an artist who is familiar with the creatures he creates. But then of course he would be, for this is his own native wildlife. Maybe one day, when our own artists learn to love muntjac, we shall see more such art from them too.

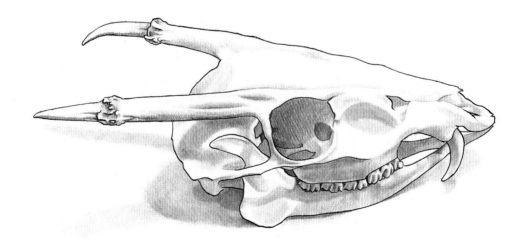

USEFUL CONTACTS

British Association for Shooting and Conservation
Marford Mill
Rossett
Wrexham LL12 0HL
Tel: 01244 573000
Email: enquiries@basc.org.uk
Web: www.basc.org.uk

British Deer Society
The Walled Garden
Burgate Manor
Fordingbridge
Hampshire SP6 1EF
Tel: 01425 655434
Email: h.q@bds.org.uk
Web: www.bds.org.uk

CIC UK National Permanent Trophy Commission
Judge's Court
Waterloo Road
Shepton Mallet
Somerset BA4 5HG
Tel: 01749 343725
Email: cicuk@btinternet.com
Web: www.cictrophy.com

Countryside Alliance
367 Kennington Road
London SE11 4PT
Tel: 020 7840 9200
Email: info@countryside-alliance.org
Web: www.countryside-alliance.org

Deer Initiative
The Carriage House
Brynkinalt Business Centre
Chirk
Wrexham LL14 5NS
Tel: 01691 770888
Email: info@thedeerinitiative.co.uk
Web: www.thedeerinitiative.co.uk

Federation of Field Sports Associations of the EU (FACE)
Rue F Pelletier 82
B-1030 Brussels
Belgium
Tel: 00322 7326 900
Email: info@face.eu
Web: www.face.eu

REFERENCES AND BIBILOGRAPHY

Chapman N, Harris S, and Stanford A (1994) Reeves Muntjac *Muntiacus reevesi* in Britain, their history, spread, habitat selection, and the role of human intervention in accelerating their dispersal, *Mammal Review* Vol 24, No 3, 113-160

Chapman N and Harris S (1996) *Muntjac*, The Mammal Society & The British Deer Society

Chapman N (2005) Muntjac in Breckland, *Deer*, Vol 13, No 6

Chapman N (2007) How old is that Muntjac, *Deer*, Vol 14, No 2

Cooke A (2006) Monitoring muntjac deer *Muntiacus reevesi* and their impacts in Monks Wood National Nature Reserve, *English Nature Research Reports*, No. 681

Cooke A (2006) There are Muntjac at the Bottom of my Garden, *Deer*, Vol 13 No 11

Cooke A (2007) The Muntjac of Monks Wood, *Deer*, Vol 14 No 2

Cooke A (2013) What you see and what you don't, *Deer*, Vol 16 No 6

Cooke A (2014) Muntjac in the Woodlands of Western Cambridgeshire, 1994-2013, *Deer*, Vol 16 No 10

Collini G (2004) Calling Muntjac, *Deer*, Vol 13 No 3

Collini G (2010) Calling all Muntjac, *Deer*, Vol 15 No 7

Downing G (2010) *Practical Woodland Stalking*, Quiller Publishing

Downing G (2013) *The Deer Stalking Handbook*, 3rd Edition, Quiller Publishing

Fletcher J (2014) *Deer*, Reaktion Books

Lever C (2009) *The Naturalized Animals of Britain and Ireland*, New Holland Publishers (UK)

Major A P, The Muntjac Deer in England, *Gamekeeper and Countryside*, January 1968

Marshall P and McCormick A (2006) *Deer Stalking Survey, A survey of BASC members' deer stalking activities*, British Association for Shooting and Conservation

Pearce I (2009) The Ghost Muntjac, *Deer*, Vol 15 No 2

Smith-Jones C (2004) *Muntjac – Managing an Alien Species*, Coch-Y-Bonddu Books

Smith-Jones C (2008) Muntjac – Use and Abuse, *Deer*, Vol 14 No 7

Wilson C J (2003), *Current and Future Deer Management Options*, Defra European Wildlife Division

INDEX